The Journey of
Intense Quietness

Also by Joan B. Weller

The Life-Giver
Betwixt and Between
In the Midst of the Fray

The Journey
of
Intense Quietness

A New Way to Live

JOAN B. WELLER

WestBow
P R E S S
A DIVISION OF THOMAS NELSON

WestBow Press books may be ordered through booksellers or by contacting:

WestBow Press
A Division of Thomas Nelson
1663 Liberty Drive
Bloomington, IN 47403
www.westbowpress.com
1-(866) 928-1240

Because of the dynamic nature of the Internet, any web addresses or links contained in this book may have changed since publication and may no longer be valid. The views expressed in this work are solely those of the author and do not necessarily reflect the views of the publisher, and the publisher hereby disclaims any responsibility for them.

Any people depicted in stock imagery provided by Thinkstock are models, and such images are being used for illustrative purposes only.
Certain stock imagery © Thinkstock.

Cover painting titled Summer at Patricks, © 2001 by Robert Weller.

ISBN: 978-1-4497-4451-9 (hc)
ISBN: 978-1-4497-4452-6 (sc)
ISBN: 978-1-4497-4453-3 (e)
Library of Congress Control Number: 2012905538

Unless otherwise noted, the Bible version used in this book is The New King James Version. Copyright @ 1979, 1980, 1982, Thomas Nelson, Inc., Publishers.

The Amplified bible (AMP) Old Testament copyright @ 1965, 1987 by The Zondervan Corporation, Grand Rapids, MI. The Amplified New Testament copyright@ 1958, 1987 by Lockman Foundation, La Habra, CA 90631.

The Living Bible (TLB) copyright 1971 by Tyndale House Publishers, Wheaton, Ill.

The Message. Copyright @1993, 1994, 1995, 1996. NavPress Publishing Group, P.O. Box 35001, Colorado Springs, CO 80933.

Printed in the United States of America
WestBow Press rev. date: 04/10/2012

Contents

Part I: Father-Tuned

The Beginning 3
A New Way to Live

Conversation 7
Revelation of Inner Life

Listen And Hear.. 11
Is Anyone Listening?

Part II: The Journey

Tribulation 17
The Valley of the Shadow of Death

Bittersweet... 23
Love Permeates Grief

Emotional Calm 27
I Will Give You Rest

The Quiet Place 31
Seedbed of Wonder and Imagination

Gentleness 35
You Are Gentle

The Walk 39
Alone with the Lord

Part III: Discovery

Discernment... 47
The Gift of the Holy Spirit

Truth 52
   Living with Truth

Ease 57
   My Yoke Is Easy, My Burden Is Light

Come! 62
   Gracious Invitation

The Gleaner 69
   Obtaining Spiritual Food

Follow Me 72
   The Way to the Father

Part IV: Intimacy

Struggle 79
   Questions, Questions, Questions

Indwelling 82
   Christ in You, the Hope of Glory

Spiritual Hunger 87
   Longing and Loneliness

Shepherd Chasing 92
   Leaving Home

Love—To Give 96
   God's Overflowing, Creative Passion

Father Love 101
   Love That Embraces and Welcomes the Lost

Part V: Responsive Obedience

Obedience 107
   Run to Do His Will

Kindness 111
   Kiss the Wound

Compassion 115
   To Suffer With

Be Honest 120
    Compassion One Side of Love—Truth the Other

Resurrection Life... 124
    Continue in Prayer

Endurance 128
    Go up Higher

Part VI: Focus

The Seeking Heart 135
    That I May Know Him

In His Presence.. 140
    Joy Unspeakable and Full of Glory

Oneness... 144
    Woven Together

Acknowledgments

I am blessed to have friends and family who love God and live by the power of the Holy Spirit. I love being with them as we learn great lessons from the Holy Spirit.

During the writing of this work, our oldest grandson, twenty-year-old Adam Garland, died suddenly of natural causes. I share with you in *The Journey of Intense Quietness* our terrible loss. During this time of grief, Jesus came to our family in the form of loving, caring, praying people. Thank you so much for being there for our daughter, son-in-law, and their five remaining children.

Special thanks go to Dee Ann Coussens and Marie Heaton for their great editorial suggestions. Thank you, Bob, for your proofreading. For those of you who read the unfinished manuscript and shared with me your feedback, thank you. I'm grateful for all your prayers and encouragement.

Part I

Father-Tuned

Welcome to *The Journey of Intense Quietness*. We have an exciting trip ahead of us. You know, don't you, that the Lord will come with us on this journey. We will experience things totally beyond the ordinary yet mixed right into everyday life.

As we journey together, dear friend, I hope your hunger for the Lord will increase and your desire to know Jesus and the Father will become the passion of your life.

As we traverse this pathway, we will have a sense of peace energized with joy. The path leads through hushed, still places and along quiet byways leading to the Father. Jesus traveled this exact way as He listened and conversed with His Father.

Chapter One

The Beginning
A New Way to Live

I will give you treasures of darkness and hidden riches
in secret places, that you may know that I, the Lord,
who called you by your name,
I am the God of Israel.

—Isaiah 45:3

Today, August 2010, I begin the actual writing of *The Journey of Intense Quietness.*

It's a beautiful mid-August day—blueberries are ripe; most of the wheat has been threshed, and the hay cut. Thank goodness it's cool and cloudy after several days of scorching heat. This morning, two does with their spotted fawns walked gracefully through the orchard, nibbling the limbs of the plum and apple trees. A coyote snuck across the meadow in front of the house on its way to the creek. As I watered my potted flowers, a green-and-orange frog popped right out of the watering pipe, surprised by the sudden shower. We are enjoying garden vegetables and the fruit, wild blackberries, and hazelnuts found in our meadow.

Without the Lord's encouragement I wouldn't have attempted to write this book. However, the Lord clearly asked me years ago to keep a record of this wondrous journey in my journal so I could share my discoveries with others. It is in the intimacy of intense quietness that I have gradually become Father-tuned as

I've learned to listen to the Spirit, paid attention to His Word, and quieted my soul.

I heard the phrase *intense quietness* for the first time on a quiet night walk with Triple Gold, my dog. That night I began the journey that opened to me hidden riches in secret places.

The Genesis of Intense Quietness

One quiet night in 1994, it was time for me to take Triple, our golden retriever, out for his dutiful walk. The night was dark and clear, without clouds or moon. In the house I clipped Triple on lead and headed down the back stairs. As we reached the bottom, he suddenly stopped, his front legs stiffened, and his ruff came up, making him look lion-like. His growl was a deep, menacing rumble. Gripping his collar, I stood rooted to the ground while his growl continued. My heart was pounding; my hair stood on end. Something was in the tree to our left. Slowly we backed up the steps and into the house. *Whoa, what was that?* I thought. *Raccoon? Owl? Housecat? Bobcat? Cougar?* My imagination ran wild.

Waiting in the house for a few minutes, we cautiously ventured out the front door and across the meadow, this time being careful to stay away from the trees. Triple was his usual happy self, not acting threatened in any way.

I love these nightly excursions, finding it fun to be without flashlight, seeing things by starlight or by the faint light from the city twenty miles away. When we came to the end of the path, Triple stopped and stood quietly at point, taking in the smells, sights, and sounds of night. With cocked ears and twitching nose he stood still, alert, watching for any motion in the shadows and trees. I'm sure he could have heard a mouse running across the grass or a gopher digging underfoot. Alert yet at ease, his nose was up, his nostrils flared, his head moved ever so slightly to catch the scent of deer half a mile away or the neighbor's cat prowling about for field mice.

It was then that an absolutely clear thought dropped into my mind:

Watch the dog. Pay attention! I want you to learn intense quietness.
What? What do You mean?
Once again the Lord spoke:
Intense quietness is being alert yet not afraid. It is an attitude of the heart in which you are aware, observant, listening, and enjoying all life. Right now, listen to the night sounds. What do you hear?

Rushing sound of water in the ravine.
Sighing of fir trees touched by a gentle breeze.
Calling of owls to each other—*whoo-whoo-whoooo* and an answering
   whoo-whoo-whoo-whooo-whoooo in a higher tone.
Barking dogs across the valley.
The low, rumbling vibration of a train engine, and then its whistle.

Now what do you see?

The vague outline of Triple.
The pathway back to the house.
The black images of the trees.

Look up!
O My Lord—stars, millions of them, galaxies, universes!
What do you hear inside your heart?

Wonder, awe, worship, thanksgiving.
Ah, Lord, I see and know so little. I'm blind and deaf.

Intense quietness is learning to hear My voice, observing what is going on around you, and listening to My Spirit. I will teach you to wait, be still, and enjoy seeing beyond the ordinary. You will learn to pay attention when warned of danger. You will understand your blindness. Your spirit will be guided by My Spirit.

The Implications

Even though I heard the Lord say these words, I really didn't understand the implications. At first I foolishly thought this quietness meant spending a little time with Jesus, but that wasn't it at all.

In the Gospel of John I found my example of how to live my life in a totally new way. I noticed Jesus always had His Spirit open to the Father and was never without tender, loving direction. He was empowered, given discernment, loved without restraint, and strengthened as He completed His holy task of redemption. He lived to please the Father. The Father was well pleased with the beloved Son.

The Question

With this insight in mind, I asked myself, *Is it possible for me to be Father-tuned, living constantly aware and listening to the Spirit, having the inner spiritual place within me open, and "hearing" the Father's voice?*

The Lord quite miraculously answered my heartfelt question by whispering His loving directions into my spirit. I gradually learned to be intensely quiet and become aware of His presence.

———

O Lord, I'm overwhelmed and thankful for Your constant love, and I desire each day to live in this intimate relationship with You.

As you prepare to share what you have learned, as you review your journals, don't become overwhelmed, but remember my simple imperatives: Listen. Come. Watch. Rejoice. Write. Walk. Rest. Love.

This book, although serious in nature, must be filled with joy and humor.

The Father will be seen.
The Son will be heard.
The Spirit will rejoice!

Chapter Two

Conversation
Revelation of Inner Life

My soul, wait silently for God alone,
For my expectation is from Him.
He only is my rock and my salvation;
He is my defense;
I shall not be moved.
—Psalm 62:5-6

August 12, 2009—I'm procrastinating. Instead of writing, I find it easier to do the chores, start dinner, and pick berries. After months of researching, organizing my material, and spending hours on prayer and thought, it is time to settle down and write *Intense Quietness.*

Lord, help!

My challenge is to share my spiritual journey in an honest and open manner. I want others to join the conversation and enter into an invisible, vital reality of spiritual life that is from the Lord.

Many books have been written about religious life; I've read a number of them. Some authors explore the discipline of daily Bible reading and prayer. Others describe the spiritual environment in which spiritual life may take place: silence, solitude, simplicity of lifestyle, and religious sacramental life. Practical exercises are recommended in order to accomplish spiritual growth. I've tried to follow their advice and do the things suggested. However, as I try to follow these disciplines I often feel bereft, loaded down with things to do, principles to follow, or ways to read the Bible. There have been only a few authors who have assisted me in experiencing life with the living, present Lord.

———

My deepest desire is to come to know and love You, Lord. I want to have conversations with You in which I hear Your ideas and thoughts, Your creative instruction, and Your glorious take on things. I want to talk with You and enjoy Your presence. Is this possible?

———

I've noticed the entire Bible is conversation between God and His people. Each book tells the story of a real, forthright God and people's responses to His presence. Some books record historical events; others tell of heroes and villains. These forthright stories convey hundreds of years of conversations with the Lord. Heartache, wickedness, violence, rebellion, betrayal, and immoral behavior are not covered up. The entire Bible is revelation, a revelation of a living God, my God, who loves and cares, disciplines and forgives, gives and comforts.

I particularly love the Book of Psalms because almost every psalm is a conversation. It is as if I can listen in on the psalmist's prayer, hear the songs, and feel the joy or despair. The language is vernacular, the pleas are open and passionate, and the complaints boil out of frustration. The psalmist, often desolate and hostile, angry and unbelieving, yells at God, asking Him questions about injustice and suffering. Then at other times I hear his expressions of love for his God, his magnificent worship, and his brilliant poetry.

In fact, this ancient prayer book is a model of all prayer, all intimate conversation with God, the God of Israel. There is no prissy, correct, polite language here; the conversation is raw and honest—so refreshing. I can relate to it on every level.

Jesus, the Book of Psalms is the prayer book of Your people and must have been Yours as well. As I read them, I sometimes can overhear You speaking the words of the psalms as You converse with Your Father. It would be great if I could share my personal conversations and experiences with You just as the writers of the psalms did.

However, I'm conflicted, hesitant to open up my journals and share the exchange of love between us. Will doing so cheapen the special moments we share? Will our sacred times together be exposed, no longer mine alone, open to criticism from those who don't know You or don't understand you?

Maybe my hesitation has to do with my cynicism. I'm often skeptical when someone says, "The Lord said this to me." Are my quiet conversations with You figments of my imagination?

I know from experience and I'm absolutely convinced Your specific directives are incredibly powerful, words that order my life. My values, my desires, my thoughts are based on a simple belief that what You say, whether directly from Scripture or spoken into my spirit, is true. Believing that, my life has been filled with twists and turns and adventures galore, some fun, others scary, and still others rich and fruitful. I'm often strengthened by Your words, and at other times I'm brought to tears by Your tender, merciful loving-kindness.

Writing *Intense Quietness* is Your assignment for me. So Lord, I need to get on it. Show me how to write of experiences gained as I learned a focused quietness filled with Your life.

Share our conversations. For instance, if I said, "Come!" what would you do?

Well Lord, my immediate reaction might be, "No, not now."

Then the questions would start:

What do You mean? Where are You? Is this Your voice? At some point, hopefully I would get it—oh, now I see. Within the word *come* is invitation.

Come, come close, and enjoy being with Me.

Along with the invitation is instruction.

Come and learn.
Come and rest.
Come and listen.
Come and follow.
Come and forgive.

I would come! There is always an expected response to Your invitation, isn't there?

As you write Intense Quietness, *instead of describing environment, share My words to you in the context of stories and examples, things learned and to be learned.*

A simple life-word is filled with process, never just one occurrence. My Word progressively brings more and more insight, requiring greater obedience, a small glimmer of understanding, an application, a need for change that leads to a continued struggle and more experiences.

I see. I just need to relate our conversations and my response. Thank You for helping me overcome my fear of sharing my communion with You.

Chapter Three

Listen And Hear
Is Anyone Listening?

Listen carefully to Me, and eat what is good,
And let your soul delight itself in abundance.
Incline your ear, and come to Me.
Hear, and your soul shall live;
And I will make an everlasting covenant with you—
The sure mercies of David.
—Isaiah 55:2-3

August 2009—the longer I live, the more I realize the Christian life is about hearing God's Spirit and then responding to what He says. I'm so saddened that in this day and age, in this culture, the ability to concentrate on the real but often hidden event of God's active presence has often taken a back seat to busyness. The primary focus seems to be on doing, accomplishing, acquiring position and things, and being entertained. There is no space for silence; inner quietness rarely occurs. God may be ready and willing to share His insight and wisdom, His plans and answers to our daily dilemmas, but confusion and noise fill the day; attention and imagination are held captive by electronic wizardry.

While reading in the Book of Isaiah, I came to a scripture that describes this poverty of spirit. Although addressed to Israel and Judah, I know this scripture is true for our time as well.

You've Seen A Lot, But Looked At Nothing

Pay attention! Are you deaf?
> Open your eyes! Are you blind?
You're my servant, and you're not looking!
> You're my messenger, and you're not listening!
The very people I depended upon, servants of God,
> Blind as a bat—willfully blind!
You've seen a lot, but looked at nothing.
> You've heard everything, but listened to nothing.
God intended, out of the goodness of his heart,
> To be lavish in his revelation.
But this is a people battered and cowed,
> Shut up in attics and closets,
Victims licking their wounds,
> Feeling ignored, abandoned.
But is anyone out there listening?
Isaiah 42:18-23, *The Message*

Lord, how sad that hardly anyone pays attention. You are hidden in the chaos of daily life, Your presence not recognized or experienced. Longed for, yes, but in actuality to many, You are a mirage—in sight but unreachable. Your constant, gentle, comforting yet strong Spirit-Word is heard infrequently, and often not at all. Prayer becomes man's monologue. Thanksgiving and petitions pour forth, and then it's time to go and get to gettin'. You listen and have things to say in reply, but by then no one is on the phone.

O Lord, this should not be.

The point of all prayer, of giving thanks and asking for help and provision, is to become better acquainted with the Lord.

There is nothing more precious and more sacred than being in His presence and having personal conversations with Him. I can only imagine His pain as He waits for His children to come and be with Him. It seems to me He is often treated as some treat their own parents. Such parents long to see and hear from their grown children, but these children rarely take time to really know the very ones who gave them life.

In the hurry and scurry of modern life, many think they know the Lord yet have never had a conversation with Him. They believe He came to earth, lived a perfect and good life, died, and rose from the dead; they are convinced Jesus is the Christ. However, I don't think reading about Him or listening to others talk about Him is the same as having a real relationship with Him.

In any relationship, the sharing of thoughts and feelings is absolutely essential for there to be a vital, living friendship; if there is no communication, there is no relationship.

Jesus spoke to His disciples of a totally new way to be with Him: "A little while longer and the world will see Me no more, but you will see Me. Because I live, you will live also. At that day you will know that I am in My Father, and you in Me, and I in you" (John 14:19).

A few years later Paul wrote this prayer to the church in Ephesus:

> May He grant you out of the rich treasury of His glory to be strengthened and reinforced with mighty power in the inner man by the Holy Spirit (Himself indwelling your innermost being and personality). May Christ through your faith (actually) dwell (settle down, abide, make His permanent home) in your hearts! May you be rooted deep in love and founded securely on love (Ephesians 3:16–17, *Amplified Bible*).

Jesus, as I came to recognize Your presence within my spirit, my spiritual ears and eyes opened. I could hear spiritual language. It was then our conversations began. Thank You for living inside of me—so marvelous, so real, and so intimate.

My dear little friend, you have obediently gathered and stored My insights. Share these with My friends. There is a tragic spiritual famine. My loved ones are hungry. Many have never experienced the silence filled with life. They do not hear Me speak, do not recognize what I'm doing, and do not carry the burden of My heart. As in times of old they see and do not perceive, hear and do not comprehend what is spoken. Many hear voices that are not mine. Ideas and principles are discussed and philosophies abound, yet all this human effort does not nourish the spirit. My personal, specific instructions fall upon deaf ears. As a result my people are restless and angry, and many have stopped talking with Me. I miss them.

Now get to work. Share The Journey of Intense Quietness. *My friends need to once again take time to listen to Me.*

Part II

The Journey

No one knows when dramatic change will occur, when life will become filled with grief and difficulty. Two weeks after I began the actual writing of *The Journey of Intense Quietness*, our family was struck with a series of tragic events. I was able to write of these in my journal. You, dear reader, will be able to read these entries.

Weep with us as we mourn the death of Adam, our oldest grandson. See the Lord's gracious presence during fearful days of sickness. Rejoice with us as we experience answers to prayer.

Come with me into intense quietness as I receive comfort from the One who is all comfort.

Chapter Four

Tribulation
The Valley of the Shadow of Death

These things I have spoken to you, that in Me
you may have peace.
In the world you will have tribulation;
but be of good cheer,
I have overcome the world.
—John 16:32-33

August 15, 2009—No one knows when dramatic change will occur, when life will become filled with sadness and difficulty. Our season of tribulation began on this day with a phone call from our son Jonathan, the youngest of our four grown children—Molly, Jason, Ben, and Jonathan.

He called from California, having returned two weeks earlier from Costa Rica; we were excited to hear from him. Little did we anticipate his alarming news.

"Hey Dad and Mom, I've been really sick since the end of July. In late afternoon I have a high fever and a splitting headache. My neck and chest lymph nodes are enlarged. The doctors don't know what is wrong but suspect a tropical disease of some kind. They've taken tubes and tubes of blood for tests. Don't worry, Mom. I just want you guys to pray."

I'm told not to worry. Hmmm—sounds pretty serious to me.

A week later—August 22, 2009—the phone rings. It's Jonathan.

"Mom and Dad?" There is a long pause. "I don't have an infection." He is crying and panicky. "The oncologist says most likely I have lymphoma. They'll know after next week what kind of lymphoma it is. I'm scheduled for a bone marrow biopsy and more scans next week. Please pray for Cindy and the boys."

We are shocked. The news could hardly be worse.

———

O Lord, no words, only groans and tears are possible. Help me stay in a place of peace. I'm terrified, helpless, and inconsolable. Our youngest son is gravely ill; You alone can be with him. He is Your beloved one, the son filled with songs and poetry, rhythm and music from the eternal realm. God, You know my anguish. All day long I hear my heartbeat in my ear; I'm afraid. Did Abraham weep for Isaac as he led him up the mountain to be sacrificed? Help us contend for his life. He is an incredible gift. Please, dear Lord, heal him. He has always been Your child; I once again release him to You. O Lord. O Lord. Cover him with Your grace. Be very close to his little boys and his much-loved wife.

———

> Because of the voice of the enemy . . .
> My heart is sore pained within me . . .
> The terrors of death are fallen upon me,
> And horror has overwhelmed me.
> Fearfulness and trembling . . .
> O that I had wings . . .
> I would wander far off . . .
> And remain in the wilderness,
> I would hasten my escape from the windy storm and
> tempest . . .

I will cry aloud . . .
And He shall hear me" (from Psalm 55).

———

Sunday Afternoon, August 24, 2009—the phone rings once again. Joshua, our sixteen-year-old grandson, is on the line.

"You need to come *now!*"
"What is it? Josh, what's the matter?"
"Adam just died."

O Lord, O Jesus.

Our oldest grandson, twenty-year-old Adam, Don and Molly's oldest son, Joshua's brother, went to bed at a friend's home Saturday night and never woke up, dying in his sleep.

Oh, the loss, the loss. He is gone—just gone.

Bob and I rush into town and are with the brokenhearted family. We walk together into the shadowed valley of death. Our dear, dear daughter and son-in-law suffer pain beyond description. Adam's brothers and sisters are inconsolable.

Crying, I call our three sons. There are shocked silences on the phone, then sobs. Oh, the grief, the tears for their sister and for the loss of Adam.

Death brings desolation. Time stands still. The atmosphere is grim. No one talks; people come and go. Grief-stricken, our daughter weeps; Don is silent, stony-faced.

Evening, August 24—In the deep place in my heart there is a song. The first words are "There's no greater love than Jesus; there's no greater love than He gives." Those words and melody run through my spirit over and over again. I know this is the Spirit singing over me. Clinging to the truth of these words, I finally sleep.

August 25—I awaken and have the words to a poem.

Grief Traveler

Sorrow greets dawn light
Tears and sighs,
Heartache and anguish.

We love and laugh and hope
As quick as the flip of the coin
The child is gone.

Sorrow and shock grip us
Tears overflow then
Ebb away to silent sobs.

Death laughs and torments.

———

Lord, I know the way through this lonely, heartbreaking wilderness is to receive Your love. In Your place of sheltering presence healing takes place.

It is difficult to concentrate; my thoughts go from the terrible grief over our grandson's death back to the frightful news of Jonathan's illness. As I awaken in the early morning, it is here, away from the grief of the family and the terrifying news of our son, that You are close. You quietly reassure me.

Death does not have the upper hand!

Your love touches my fearful soul. I long for comfort, but the surface of my heart is as stone. I absolutely know You are present and in charge even though I do not feel any solace or peace or hope.

———

Our family is known and loved. The Spirit speaks into the hearts of family, neighbors, friends, and the community.

Pray! Come! Gather! Cry! Embrace! Comfort! Give! Speak My Word! Do the things that will help!

Beloved friends and family hear the Lord's imperatives and respond. They contend and weep, call and provide. The Body of Christ, visible for these long hard days, is truly the Lord's expression of love that pours into our wounds and broken hearts.

August 26—Another call from Jonathan. "Mom, I'm just bummed. I want to be up there with Molly, but there's no way I can come. I'm scheduled for a bone marrow biopsy later this week. They are running hundreds of tests for tropical diseases and cancer markers. I'm having another scan today, and they have scheduled a nuclear scan down at Berkeley this coming weekend. I'm still running the fever with headache in the late afternoon. They have checked repeatedly for malaria, and so far all the tests are negative. Next week they're doing surgery to biopsy the lymph nodes in my chest cavity."

August 30—The day of the funeral. Many friends and family, some driving hundreds of miles just to be with us at Adam's funeral, gather to say goodbye to Adam, a tenderhearted and loving young man. No words can express the loss. The firstborn son is dead.

The service celebrates the hope of resurrection because of Jesus' sacrifice. Then it is over. Life is precious; the loss enormous. Raw grief, wailing and sighs, one last touch of the beloved son—then the casket is closed.

As we drive to the gravesite, the clouds darken, boiling over the hill. At the cemetery the rain begins as the doleful sound of the bagpipe accompanies the burial.

"I am the resurrection and the life," says the Lord; "he that believes in Me, though he were dead, yet shall he live . . ."

"We commit Adam's body to the ground; earth to earth, ashes to ashes, dust to dust . . ."

Unfolding Grace

The Lord invades terror;
The miraculous pours into bitter grief.
Love embraces sorrow;
Truth mingles with despair.
Revelation fractures frozen images;
Perfect Love weeps with us.
Soon Peace enters times of sleep;
Restoration begins.

This is the journey; tribulation is part of life.
Surrounded by intense quietness, I weep.

Chapter Five

Bittersweet

Love Permeates Grief

How blessed the man you train, God,
The woman you instruct in your Word,
Providing a circle of quiet within the clamor of evil . . .

If God hadn't been there for me,
I never would have made it.
The minute I said, "I'm slipping; I'm falling,"
Your love, God, took hold and held me fast.
When I was upset and beside myself,
You calmed me down and cheered me up.
—Psalm 94, *The Message*

September 1, 2009, early morning—Molly calls.

"Mom and Dad?" Her voice is flat and weary. "I spent the night in the emergency room with Joshua (Molly and Don's sixteen-year-old son). He has meningitis and is in the pediatric isolation unit at St. Vincent's Hospital."

I can hardly believe this. "Oh, honey, we'll come right away."

Oh, Jesus, please dear Lord, heal him.

I call our friends once again for prayer; they cannot believe this is happening.

We immediately leave for the hospital. When we arrive, we find out the doctors have just determined Joshua has viral, not bacterial, meningitis, which is much better news. He'll be in the hospital for a few days and then home for the first two weeks of school.

Oh, Lord, please no long-term effects.

Evening, September 1, 2009—Jeni (the wife of Jason, our oldest son) calls from Washington.

"Hi . . . I thought you should know Jason is in the hospital in Walla Walla. He came down with the flu after returning from Molly's. He has pneumonia and is dehydrated, and his blood sugars are very high."

I'm in shock. I really can't believe this—the spiritual attack is over the top.

"Jen, thanks for calling. We'll be praying; I'm so sorry we can't be with you with all the family emergencies here. Call us if he doesn't respond to treatment."

Oh, Lord, please heal Jason and comfort Jeni and relieve her fear.

Anguish pervades every moment. Adam is dead, and nothing will bring him back. Joshua and Jonathan are gravely ill, and Jason has pneumonia. What's next?

Lord, I know within each tragic event there is always Your presence, a tender display of pure grace. It remains a wonder that even in the middle of sorrows Your gentle love permeates the grief. Into the somber weaving of black and brown, gray and midnight blue are threads of bright red, gold, and azure.

Priorities have changed. What seemed important—the chores, the routine, the dog, the weather and news, the little things—are not even on the list. Now we are with family, staying available for anything needed. I call in the troops for prayer and thank them for their care and thoughtfulness. People even come out to our house hugging us, bringing food, praying for the entire family.

Life seems more precious than before. Seeing our children, just looking into each of their faces, brings tears. I want to linger in their hugs. I find myself treasuring memories of their growing-up years, funny episodes of laughter when we were all together. Just to think any one of the children or grandchildren might not be here tomorrow brings inner groans and protests. Adam's death is real yet unacceptable. I can no longer count on tomorrow; today is the only opportunity to say "I love you."

Sorrow enlarges my heart and makes me extremely thankful for tender acts of kindness. Hugs bring much comfort. Friends are extraordinarily important. Compassionate tears from others help lift the heaviness. Time seems to slow down and almost stop.

———

I'm incredibly grateful to you, dear Lord, for Your constant presence all during these long, hard days.

I find myself strangely alert and emotionally open, able to enjoy the simplest things.
I hear a beautiful tune whistled by a stranger in the grocery store.
I see sunshine break through clouds.
I taste hot, bitter coffee.
I touch the soft, furry ears of my dog Cricket.
I smell spicy apple butter simmering on the stove.

An old Irish melody runs through my "singer," an ancient prayer—for each day:

> Lord of all hopefulness, Lord of all joy
> Whose trust ever childlike, no care could destroy.
> Be there at our waking, and give us, we pray,
> Your bliss in our hearts, Lord, at the break of the day.
>
> Lord of all eagerness, Lord of all faith

Whose strong hands were skilled at the plane and the
    lathe,
Be there at our labors, and give us we pray
Your strength in our hearts, Lord, at the noon of the day.

Lord of all kindliness, Lord of all grace
Your hands swift to welcome, Your arms to embrace,
Be there at our homing, and give us, we pray,
Your love in our hearts, Lord, at the eve of the day.

Lord of all gentleness, Lord of all calm,
Whose voice is contentment, whose presence is balm,
Be there at our sleeping, and give us we pray
Your peace in our hearts, Lord, at the end of the day.[1]

From the dark, shadowed valley of death, joy begins a slow, graceful dance with sorrow. I've been here before. I know healing may be slow in coming, but it comes. The song of hope never ends.

---

[1]   Jan Struther, *The Hymnal of the Protestant Episcopal Church* (New York: The Church Pension Fund, 1940), p.363.

Chapter Six

Emotional Calm

I Will Give You Rest

It is good that one should hope and wait quietly for
the salvation of the Lord.
—Lamentations 3:26

October 22, 2009—Chilly mornings, wispy fog in the valley,
red and yellow apples ready for harvest, bright red dogwood seeds
providing feasts for woodpeckers, robins, and flickers—October
is here.

Yesterday, when I came out of the house, at least twenty
robins were lawn hopping, listening, hopping—worm hunting.
Two bright blue stellar jays scolded me from the hazelnut tree,
a chipmunk scurried across my path, and a red-bellied squirrel
chattered from the woods. I noticed the little house wrens were
back for the winter. So far there has been no noisy flyover of ducks
and geese on their way south—but soon. The rains will come; a
cold wind will howl down the gorge.

This morning I must take time, settle down, and write.
September and the first part of October whizzed by. It seems
forever since Adam died. Relative calm has returned, yet grief takes
its great toll. Tiny tasks are difficult; getting anything done seems
impossible. It seems like my "car" is stuck in neutral. Sorrow makes
it hard to focus. Thoughts shuffle through my mind and then shift
to others and then drift to "What if" and "I should." Even my

dreams are filled with vivid, emotional episodes of weeping, anger, fear, and confusion. Fatigue, frequent tears, and thankfulness mix.

———

Lord, even though You have been present during every day, I find it hard to tune in to Your Word and receive comfort. I sense the devilish onslaught has stopped. I'm so thankful for Your constant love. So many people have prayed and carried us during this time of grief. You have certainly answered prayer in a spectacular way.

Good News!

Joshua has recovered from meningitis without any long-lasting effect, and Jason is over the flu and doing well.

The best news of all—Jonathan doesn't have cancer! After countless blood tests, scans, and bone marrow and lymph node biopsies, his tests are negative for lymphoma or any other cancer. At this time the puzzled doctors have made no definitive diagnosis. Without any medical intervention at all, Jon is feeling better; however, the lymph nodes in his chest are still swollen. The hope is the swelling will diminish; the doctors plan to monitor him until all symptoms are gone. If he relapses, they will send him to Stanford University Medical School for further tests for unusual infections and autoimmune disorders, but for now, thank goodness, he is symptom-free. I'm so relieved. What tremendously good news this is. Yes! Thanks, Lord!

———

Father, You know when Jonathan first called with the original diagnosis I was distraught, imagining the disastrous days ahead for him and his family. Yet in those desperate moments You, Lord, seemed to whisper, *He is healing.*

Sorry to say I dismissed those words as just wishful thinking and did not believe that quiet declaration bouncing across my confused mind and raw emotions. The horrific circumstance seemed totally real. I was afraid to believe. My soul was mightily distressed, filled with fear and sorrow. I'm so glad in this case You, dear Lord, healed him in spite of my unbelief.

Even though I felt blind and deaf to what the Lord was doing, my spirit was and is strangely quiet, at rest. Under all the emotional commotion, in my inner heart I can sense the Spirit, who is settled and confident. This quietness is not passivity or peace but an expectant attitude of "Wait, be still, and see what will happen." Ah! Intense quietness!

Intense quietness does not come naturally. I find it hard to wait, watch, and listen. It seems like nothing is happening, no one is listening, all is falling apart. I know in my mind it is stupid to think I have much effect at all on illness, death, sorrow, pain, or captivity. My fretting and worry are desperate ploys to control the circumstances.

Lord, I know that only as I release my loved ones to Your care do I gain confidence You are at work and fixin' things. Then I'm able to rest, wait, and watch as You restore and comfort, heal and strengthen. It is in this letting go, this relinquishing, that I gain the ability to hear and see your great, embracing love. My soul may be dis-eased, quite sure things are out of control and horrific, but my spirit is filled with health and ease, aware that these awful circumstances are only a small part of reality. Waiting, watching, listening to Your Spirit is how I'll come to see more of the real picture. Out of sorrow, joy will return; out of despair, hope will come; out of death, life will come.

I'm reminded of Paul's final farewell as he prays for the beloved church at Ephesus: "So now, brethren, I commend you to God and to the word of His grace, which is able to build you up and give you an inheritance among all those who are sanctified" (Acts 20:32).

I'm so glad I can sit and write in my journal, recording the Lord's miraculous healing of my broken heart.

Chapter Seven

The Quiet Place

Seedbed of Wonder and Imagination

My soul waits for the Lord
More than those who watch for the morning
Yes, more than those who watch for the morning.
—Psalm 130:6

January 2010—We enjoyed a quiet Christmas celebration: singing old carols in the church service; giving and receiving simple, loving gifts and warm hugs; enjoying a tiny tree all decked out in handcrafted straw ornaments. I'm thankful that unlike last year's huge snow storm we had mild weather. There is a lingering sadness in the family.

———

Jesus, please mend the broken heart of our daughter. Let her know Your incredible healing and love. It is hard to watch the tears and hear the cries for help. All I can do is listen, intercede, and release her to Your care.

The Seedbed of Wonder and Imagination

I'm so thankful that even in childhood I had a love of quietness. I had idle time to wonder, to imagine, and to wander about. I know it was in this space of quiet time that little Joanie first experienced the Lord's gentle presence.

I love silence in the forest, on the porch, in the car, on the beach, in the garden, in my light-filled room. Even when I read about quietness, the descriptions often touch me. For instance, I found this wonderful description of quietness in a story about a schoolmaster in England, post-World War I.

> Here you could almost reach out and touch the quiet. It was a living thing that seemed to catch its breath up there in the hanging woods and then, at a wordless command, slip down the long hillside and gust over the rails to lose itself in the wood opposite. Its touch was gentle and healing, passing over his scars like fingers of a woman. He wanted to embrace it, press it into himself, swallow it, lose himself in it. And all the time the white clouds overhead kept pace with it, moving in massive formation across the blue band above the valley and the breeze smelled of resin and bracken and all manner of clean, washed, living things.[2]

I am at home in quietness. In fact, it is here that I find it easiest to hear, listen, and see in the spirit. My love of contemplation helps me quiet down so I can recognize the Lord's voice and absorb His Word. I deliberately take time away from noise and earthly conversation to be quiet, to tune into God's reality, a stream of revelation and encouragement. I look forward to this time—a space filled with peace and words, creativity and joy. I love being in the Lord's presence, enjoying and responding to His love.

One of my favorite early memories, an experience of silence, solitude, and stillness, is illustrative of this kinesthetic, quiet place. I was about five, just recovering from an ear infection, awake and

---

[2]   R. F. Delderfield, *To Serve Them All My Days* (New York: Simon and Schuster, 1972), 7

alone. Wrapping a blanket around my skinny little body, I sat on the wooden windowsill and watched the coming of day. In the predawn darkness, the fog had settled in along the river and on the town. The silence was absolute; the fog muted even birdsong. Floating here and there, the mist blocked the warm light of the street lamps.

Gradually, darkness turned to predawn light. The whirring of bicycle wheels broke the silence. The newspaper boy whizzed by out of the fog on his way up to the neighbors on the hill behind our house, and then returned on his way to his next delivery. Next, I heard the squeal of truck brakes just beyond the fog curtain. The milkman materialized, carrying two one-quart bottles of milk that he put on the back stairs.

Daybreak came with birdsong; sunshine changed the shadowed driveway into clover greens and gravel blues. My vivid imagination was filled with make-believe things like "fairies living in the clover patches." I watched to see if any of these tiny creatures flew away into the bright morning light. The sun finally won out over the cool fog, striking the window with warmth. I hummed a little tune. Oh, how I loved this quietness and the warmth of the morning sun.

In this stillness I remember feeling sad and afraid. The sadness was probably caused by my mother's loneliness (my dad was interned in the Philippines as a Japanese prisoner of war). I was especially afraid at night when the blackout sirens went off. Leaving my sister and me alone in the dark house, Mother left to serve on the civil defense team. I would become terrified, believing the "Japs" were coming to get us. (Even today that peculiar siren sound gives me the shivers.) The fear left as the morning sun warmed me; I felt secure and comforted.

In this peaceful stillness I believe I first sensed the Lord's presence. It was not in the sense of seeing Him or hearing Him, but in a profound stillness. As I sang and talked to myself, I started communing with my heavenly Father. These early conversations were the genesis of prayer. It was many years later before I realized that quietness, open vulnerability, and childlike wonder are the very beginnings of spiritual life.

———

As I sit in the sunshine today, writing about the quiet place, I'm so grateful. Often Your Word comes into my thoughts during this peaceful time. It might be just a phrase, a verse from Scripture, or an insight. As I reflect upon these simple, profound words whispered into my spirit, questions come. I ask them, and You gently answer me, explaining these rich and wise words. I'm amazed and filled with delight because the answers are given so tenderly. I sense Your love and mercy, wisdom and great truth-filled strength. Ah, Lord, thanks for letting me experience this quiet restful place.

Morning Moment

Crescent moon, morning star
Adorn dawn sky.
Fog hugs valley floor,
Mist-curtain teases eye.
First light strikes wet circle-webs,
Fir branches sigh, stirred by breeze
Silent moment brings
Memory of child in window
Humming a tune.

Chapter Eight

Gentleness
You Are Gentle

You have also given me the shield of Your salvation;
Your right hand has held me up,
Your gentleness has made me great.
You enlarged my path under me,
So my feet did not slip.
—Psalm 18:35-36

January 28, 2010—It's hard to concentrate today. I have several projects all needing immediate attention and discernment. Of course, my inability to focus is my own fault. I've been reading various and sundry things, trying to receive guidance about too many subjects, and it has left me confused and dissatisfied.

———

Lord, what I really need to know is what is in Your heart. Please forgive me for not taking the time to seek You, the source of all ideas, thoughts, and words. You are the One who is beyond, before and above, deeper and richer, who is Love that creates, saves, hopes, and reaches out. You alone are the point of all study. You hover over me, gently inviting me to learn Your "unforced rhythms of grace" (*The Message*). You are gentle of spirit. May I learn this gentleness.

Dear Lord, You are certainly patient. Teaching me the art of gentleness is no easy matter. Thanks for sticking with it. Your persistent, tender counsel has given me access to the inner hearts of many people. I've observed and handled treasure beyond imagining.

———

Years ago the Lord started a process that would give me a gentle spirit. I recorded one of the lessons in my journal. I'm glad I did because now I can see more clearly what I've learned.

April 2001—Last night as I was praying for a friend, I had a surprising thought: *Reach into the pool gently.*

I immediately saw in my mind's eye the pool formed by the natural spring that rises on our property. It nestles in a velvet carpet of moss and clover, almost hidden under giant ferns. The forest forms a canopy seventy-five feet overhead. The spring water is cold, clear, and luscious, filtered through eight hundred feet of sandstone. Overflowing from the pool is a tiny stream running down a ravine across our property.

Curious to really see the pool, I hiked up the hill to the spring. In the soft mud around the pool were tracks of raccoon, deer, coyote, and dog. I found several brown-and-orange salamanders, a gray frog, and of course slugs (Oregon being the slug capital of the world). A pocket gopher had left mounds of dirt on the path.

The water in the pool was still, mirroring sky and trees. Squatting down, I peered at the water and saw a slightly distorted likeness of myself. Under the surface were rocks and leaves, clay and sticks. The water was so frigid that my hand ached almost immediately as I touched the slimy maple leaves covering the bottom.

———

So Lord, what does it mean to reach into the pool gently?

Only those who reach into the pool gently will find the hidden treasure. Be patient or you will miss my gift. Do not stir the pool. Do not jump in.

I don't get it. What are You saying?

I'm already at work, carefully drawing each person to Myself. I want you to be part of the process. If you rudely enter a conversation expressing ideas, opinions, prejudices, the inner heart of that person will remain closed, and you will never find the beautiful things inside that person; you will not see the treasure. In fact, you will hinder My work.

O brother, with my exuberant personality, learning this gentleness will take forever.

I have time!

———

Thus began the lesson on gentleness.

January 28, 2010—Today I rejoice because the Lord has taught me so much. Of course, the lessons on gentleness will continue the rest of my life. I realize I've become much more relaxed and transparent. As people sense my openness and welcoming attitude, they are sometimes brave enough to reveal their thoughts and feelings. It is then I must be very gentle, sensitive, and discerning, being careful with their vulnerable and tender inner hearts. As I get to know, really know, their personal stories of triumphs and failures, they become more comfortable and relaxed. It is then their need for love allows them to reach into my inner life and find the Holy Spirit, the hidden One who lives in my spirit. They then find Peace, the One who is Peace. What a wondrous event this is. I have the great privilege of watching them drink Living Water. Strengthened, they leave refreshed, encouraged, and changed.

Not everyone is happy to be in a relationship with me. I've found that sometimes just under a friendly exterior a person may be filled with malignant hatred and aggressive anger. When I'm faced with this behavior, my first thought is, *So if you want to be this way, I'm outta here.* I've learned to step back a little to avoid getting bit by the guard dog. However, part of the lesson about gentleness is to be patient; this initial behavior frequently doesn't last.

———

Your wise instruction in this case:

Do not wrestle with the hostility
Walk alongside—be quiet
The turbulent water will settle
Watch for receptivity—my Truth will then find a home

The storm will pass
The treasure will become evident
Wait! Listen! Watch! Pray!

I know, Lord, that You have worked some of this gentleness into me. It has been painful yet such a wonder to me. Sorrow has quieted my merry heart. Grief has woven compassion into my soul. Those who are receptive to Your Spirit come forward in the presence of this sorrow; in the presence of my naturally merry heart they tend to stand back. Few can enjoy pure joy. However, if sorrow is woven together with joy, it becomes a rich, healing ointment—a precious fragrance of authenticity.

STILLNESS

Deep pool hidden in mossy carpet
Sits in floor of clover, fern
Lays open, still
Reflecting filtered sun, leaves, sky
Many stop, peer in
See image
They bow to dip, to drink, to wash
Refreshed they move away.
Wellspring stills once more.

Chapter Nine

The Walk
Alone with the Lord

I will dwell in them and walk among them.
I will be their God, and they shall be My people.
I will be a Father to you, and you shall be my sons
and daughters.
—2 Corinthians 6:16, 18

February 2010—Yesterday, when I was contemplating my afternoon walk, it was breezy and raining—not a downpour, just a light drizzle. My thoughts were, as usual, whiney—*Not today! Not now! Why bother?* Cricket (the dog) doesn't need this walk, and I have other things to do. Then I scolded myself: *Disregard this mind chatter and just go. Stop the griping.*

I put on rain gear and boots, collected my stuff: pruning clippers, water, hat, Cricket's whistle (a .30-06 shell casing), a lead, and milk bone treats. I'm off. Cricket is leaping and tearing around, a full-blown joy attack. We head down the hill, through the maple and fir trees, up the path across the neighbor's clear-cut area. The red-tail hawk screeches a greeting as he leaves his tree perch. So begins another walk . . .

My walks were the Lord's idea. When I first started this daily exercise routine, I had no idea how life-changing it would become. At the time I certainly needed to leave the comforts of the house and its routine and get some exercise for my health, for the dog's well-being, and just to get into the large, quiet, out-of-doors space. It was beautiful outside; I loved seeing the clouds, waterfalls, beaver dams, and wild critters. However, as much as I enjoyed the walks, the Lord had a totally life-changing plan for these hiking times.

———

So yesterday as I trekked along, lest I forget how important these times are, I asked,

Lord, remind me why this time is so important.

It is open space. Enter this time without agenda, time not shaped by usefulness or busyness. You are learning the rhythm of grace.

Wow! What a startling reminder—His way is not my way of thinking! I was raised believing it was sinful to fritter away time. Value was placed on relationships with family and friends or purposeful work or creative activities. Accomplishment was rewarded. Doing nothing was thought of as laziness.

When I first started walking alone, I found my thoughts were fragmented, confused, filled with tiny dramas that had little to do with anything. This mind-clutter completely distracted me from seeing or hearing anything important. Also, emotionally I felt nothing, which at the time seemed normal. After thirty years of work and ministry, marriage and child rearing, my performance-driven life had taken an emotional toll.

Week after week, as I continued my walks alone through wind and rain, my emotional numbness gradually dissipated. I discovered a deep loneliness tucked under all the busyness. It was as if getting out in open space exposed a deeper level of emotional reality. In the open space no one was there, no one cared what I did. My good performance didn't matter. Much of how I saw myself was framed by others. As I trudged on, feeling more and more alone, the tears came easily, anger flitted at the edge of my heart, hopelessness seemed ever present. I came to realize I was addicted to people and their affirmation.

Sometimes a friend came with me on these excursions. I enjoyed the good conversations and experiences. However, as great as those times were, they never lasted. When alone again, I was even more miserable. Was I addicted to people? Yep!

I have always taken comfort in the company of my dogs. There have been four: Boomer, Triple Gold, Copper, and the current one, Cricket. However, they too were often not with me. Old Boomer soon couldn't walk well enough to come along. I left him tied up on the porch. The whole neighborhood could hear his woeful howling. Next came Triple Gold, a golden retriever that became my companion. Just watching him enjoy the hikes was wonderful. Sadly, he died from cancer at an early age. Oh, oh—my sobs and tears went on for days; now I was really alone. I could hardly stand to hike without him.

———

Can I quit the walk, Lord?

No! Go alone. You have much to learn.

Every place I went reminded me of my high-spirited, wonderful dog. Oh, how I hated those lonely walks. No snow dancer, no sleeper-in-puddles, no beaver hunter, no prancing partner. I'd pray and plead with the Lord for relief but to no avail.

Slowly but surely I came to know my sorrow and loneliness were ultimately not caused by loss or absence of people or circumstances; my unhappiness was because I needed people to make me happy. When the Lord removed all companionship, I saw my deeper addiction. I was captive to having my own way, controlling the circumstances to meet my perceived need. God desired to deliver me from this addiction so I could enjoy His time schedule, His gifts of friends, His order, and most of all, His presence.

In *Growing Strong in the Seasons of Life,* Charles Swindoll describes how it is when God interferes with our perceived control:

> Being better at smothering than loving, we are blown
> away with the thought of relaxing our gargantuan
> grip. Because releasing introduces the terror of risk,

the panic of losing control. The parting cannot happen without inward bleeding. The coward heart fears to surrender its prized toys. Even though it must say goodbye eventually.

The greater the possessiveness, the greater the pain. The old miser within us will never lie down quietly and die obediently to our whisper. He must be torn out . . . he must be extracted in agony and blood like a tooth from the jaw. And we will need to steel ourselves against his piteous begging, recognizing it as echoes from the hollow chamber of self-pity, one of the most hideous sins of the human heart.

What is it God wants me to do? To hold things loosely, that He might reign without rival. With no threats to His throne and with just enough splinters in my pride to keep my hands empty and my heart warm.[3]

During this time I deeply resented the Lord for picking on me. At the time I felt it was my right to relate to anyone or anything I thought was good for me. However, I had forgotten I belonged to Him; He was claiming ownership. That was the deal when I committed my life to Him in exchange for His life, His eternal life, His abundant life. I was beginning to think everything important and everyone precious in my life would be taken away and He didn't care how I felt. Of course that was not true. Instead, He deeply cared that all my relationships were under His authority, under His keeping.

One day He gently said,

I am a jealous God! When you are with people, I walk along with you. When you are alone, you choose to walk with Me. I love to love you, comfort you, play with you, sing with you, direct you, teach you.

---

3   Charles R. Swindoll, *Growing Strong in the Seasons of Life* (Portland, Ore.: Multnomah Press, 1983), 190-191.

Oh, what a revelation! The walk was primarily for the Lord's enjoyment; I was cut to the heart. O Lord, I'm so sorry for being so angry. I never realized this walk was designed so we could have exclusive time together. Such a tenderhearted desire, and all the while I'm feeling sorry for myself.

The Walk

Fall 2000—It's getting late. I need to be out the door. "Be back in an hour."

The evening is warm. Boomer bounds off the porch, dancing away. My pace is fast. I'm a bit sad; the tears come just as I start down the straight stretch. This makes me mad. I thought—I thought I was over all these tears.

The air is layered with pockets of warm, then cool. I listen to the approaching night alive with the rhythmic vibrations of crickets and grasshoppers.

The first mile settles me down and warms me up. As I turn south, the Quiet Voice whispers,

You wanted to feel My presence, didn't you? Most of your "knowing" of Me is only head knowledge. I called you into this lonely place with Me to bring healing to your innermost being. I allowed the pain you've experienced during these lonely walks to release all the hurt tucked away under My grace. You are no longer numb. Now you feel anger, grief, fear, hatred, sorrow, and oppression. You also know times of love and tenderness, joy and happiness. You are ready for the silent place with Me.

The quiet Voice stops and is replaced with

> Fear not, for I have redeemed you; I have called you by your name; you are Mine. When you pass through the waters, I will be with you; and through the rivers, they shall not overflow you. When you walk through the fire, you shall not be burned, nor shall the flame scorch you, for I am the Lord your God, the Holy One of Israel, your Savior. (Isaiah 43:1–3)

At the top of the hill after the ravine, the air warms, the night vibrations intensify, the soft darkness descends. Boomer, my silent partner, goes on lead as night approaches. Now my heart sings, "I Was Made to Love You—I Was Made to Glorify Your Name."

Turning north, I see the beautiful little valley, a hint of pink in the west, orange in the east. The breeze is gentle. The first of the stars appear, one here, one there.

I reach a flat area where I sit on the ground, leaning on a fencepost. Boomer comes and sits on my feet. As I watch and listen darkness deepens, the Big Dipper appears in the north. Memories of many people, lonely and wondering about life just as I am, flood my thoughts.

Lord, bring comfort to the brokenhearted. You have prepared me to enter the intimate space of the beloved. I have learned so much and experienced Your goodness that is full of mercy, graciousness, long-suffering, and forgiveness. Lord, I want to be as You are.

Up the final hill, and I'm home.

To this very day *the walk* continues. Do I still feel the loneliness? Sure. However, His love for me has entered my heart and changed it. Now I share an inner chatter with Him:

Look, Lord, at that beetle. Oh, the owl, how can he fly through the tree trunks like that? The elk are down from the high ridge, must be going to snow. Wow, the bright-green moss pantaloons on the trees trunks are so neat. Aren't the sparkling water drops on the spruce boughs wonderful? On and on it goes—pure delight! Beautiful!

We walk together in the empty space through sunshine and shadow, rain and wind. I'm amazed all the time.

Part III

Discovery

Sometimes I think I know a great deal about spiritual life. Of course, this is completely egocentric and prideful, and it leads to deception. The cure for this overestimation of my spiritual insight is being with the Lord. It is very humbling, to say the least. I see and know only a little and grasp just a tiny bit of God's reality. He is gracious and loves me anyway.

As we proceed on this journey, there is a continual illumination of Word and Spirit. Underneath the life stories there is truth to be discovered.

Come on! Step along with me and enjoy the Lord who is Truth Himself.

Chapter Ten

Discernment
The Gift of the Holy Spirit

God's wisdom is something mysterious that goes deep
into the interior of his purposes. You don't find it
lying around on the surface . . . The Spirit, not content
to flit around on the surface, dives into the depths
of God, and brings out what God planned all along.
Whoever knows what you're thinking and planning
except you yourself? The same with God—except
that he not only knows what he's thinking,
but he lets us in on it.
—1 Corinthians 2:7, 10, *The Message*

Lord, what a glorious morning it is! Discovering life beyond
the ordinary—real and eternal life—starts with an awareness that
such a life exists. As I think about my experiences with You, I
realize most of what I discern of spiritual life comes from my
relationship with the Holy Spirit; You promised to send the Spirit
after Your ascension, and You did just that.

———

It is the Holy Spirit who walks with me each day, opening
my spiritual eyes and ears so I can discern God's presence. I'm

completely amazed and worship-filled as I remember how I came to know Him.

As I thought about this chapter, a long-lost childhood memory popped into my mind, a memory of my first inquiry into spiritual reality, into discernment of spiritual things.

The Memory

It's a hot summer day in Northern California. I'm ten years old, and I'm sitting in a small Methodist church listening to what I think is a long-winded sermon. I'm seriously bored and can hardly wait for the service to be over. At long last we sing the closing hymn, "In the Garden." Giggling and whispering to a friend, we laugh at old Mrs. Brown who is dressed up in her Sunday best: a floppy colorful hat, white gloves, flowered cotton dress, thick stockings, and sturdy shoes. Off-key and in a wobbly voice, Mrs. Brown devotedly sings, "I come to the garden alone, while the dew is still on the roses . . . and He walks with me and He talks with me, and He tells me I'm his own . . ." Making fun of her, I shamelessly mimic her squawky voice as I sing the last chorus.

Little did I know the Lord would use the words "He walks with me and talks with me" to catapult me upon a lifelong quest.

Beginning of Questions

Although I was rude and unashamed of my behavior that day, questions began racing through my mind. Does God personally talk with people? If that's true, then how does He do it? And if that's true, why haven't I experienced this phenomenon? Oh, my goodness, these questions led me on a path that led to all kinds of discoveries. What awesome things I've experienced.

I have always had a God-given hunger to know God. In spite of my resistance and pragmatism, I have a wonderful excitement about the things of God. As a child I was totally enthralled with the Hollywood renditions of biblical stories, so much so I couldn't sleep after seeing one of these films; I was captivated by Jesus.

In my early teens I formally received Jesus as Savior and Lord. At that time I had a simple faith, believing Jesus came to earth, died for me on the cross, and rose again.

———

Jesus, I'm eternally grateful to You for drawing me to Yourself, opening my spirit to receive the things of God: Your spectacular and precious gift of salvation and the incredible gift of the Holy Spirit. Your gentle loving-kindness, compassionate mercy, and profound righteousness and humility allowed me to see the invisible Father, the One You portray.

———

Early in my relationship with the Lord I surely needed to learn many things. I soon found I couldn't even live the Christian life as described in the Bible. The more I tried to be good and act like Jesus, the more frustrated I became.

When people personally witnessed to me, I listened to their stories and realized they were strengthened by God in the midst of terrible circumstances. There was Lula Bell and Walter, who deeply loved their Jesus. I watched Lula Bell die in perfect peace from a very painful disease. Blind, sick, courageous Tony knew each step he took every day was empowered by the Spirit as he cared for his quadriplegic wife and raised their three teenagers.

Emil and his wife Darrell, Bob and my best friends, were instrumental in our spiritual growth as they spent time teaching us to pray and to see God in the little blessings of each day. I'm thankful for the witness of these believers.

All the while my spiritual hunger continued. I was looking for the things that happened in the Bible. I finally met some believers who shared their experience of receiving the baptism in the Holy Spirit. When in their presence I could sense Jesus in the room doing His work of salvation, healing, deliverance, and answering prayer. At the time all this seemed a bit weird to me.

I found a description of the baptism in the Holy Spirit in the Bible. This phrase is first mentioned by John the Baptist as he introduced Jesus: "There is One coming who will baptize you with the Holy Spirit and fire." Well that was news to me.

My hunger increased, but so did my resistance and fear. Were these experiences of God or just some cockeyed craziness? I was afraid nothing would be different if I prayed for the baptism in the Holy Spirit. And quite the opposite, if something *did* happen, I knew my whole understanding of life would change. My life would be totally about Jesus; I would be different. What would friends and family think?

Finally, after many years of searching and struggle, my hunger overcame my fear. I asked Jesus to baptize me in the Holy Spirit. He did just that, leaving me totally immersed in the Holy Spirit. Captive to the Spirit, my life no longer belonged to me. The Spirit was in control; I now lived and moved and had my being in the Lord. What a mighty, awesome experience! (Acts 17:28)

———

I'm just amazed and so thankful that since that day, Spirit of God, You have been my constant Companion, my Comforter, my Peace, my Teacher, and my Advocate.

———

Immediately after I was baptized in the Holy Spirit, the Scriptures came alive. Prior to that I enjoyed the Bible as an amazing collection of poetry and songs, prayers and praise, history, philosophy, and ethics. After Jesus baptized me in the Holy Spirit, I spent hours devouring the Word, fascinated by the God-story, the story about His plan, His patience, His love, His judgment, His mercy, His sacrifice, His eternal kingdom.

Jesus became real not only in the stories in the Scripture but also in my everyday life. I found the Word "living and powerful, and sharper than any two-edged sword, piercing even to the division of soul and spirit, and of joints and marrow, and discerning the thoughts and intents of my heart" (Hebrews 4:12). The Spirit led me to the real treasure, the wonderful, loving God, the only One full of mercy and truth.

To this day it is the Spirit who directs my path, nudging me this way and that way, keeping me from living in my imaginary illusions. On a daily basis He gives me insights and discernment about all kinds of things. He answers my questions, letting me in on His plans. I can often see what He is doing in a situation, and He sometimes invites me to participate in the process. It is through His revelation that I have learned to love Jesus and been able to "see" the Father.

I've learned real discernment comes from the Spirit of God. He is the one who reveals what is real or unreal, true or false, wise or foolish, right or wrong, good or evil. Because He indwells me, if I tune my heart to sense His wisdom, I can often comprehend things that are obscure, the hidden thoughts and feelings in myself and others. I discover what is true, appropriate, and/or excellent. If I pay attention to His nudge, I can know when an event is Godly or of human origin.

He is the Great Gift sent from the Father and Son; I'm awestruck by their Gift.

Chapter Eleven

Truth

Living with Truth

And I will pray the Father, and He will give you
another Helper, that He may abide with you
forever—the Spirit of Truth, whom the world cannot
receive, because it neither sees Him nor knows Him;
but you know Him, for He dwells with you
and will be in you.

—John 14:16-17

June 2010—As I listen to the news and talk with people, I'm alarmed at the increasing deception that seems to be everywhere. Confusion prevails, and truth is lost among all the good intentions, careful fears, and pitiful voices of victims. I've gotten to the place where I listen with a cynical ear; nothing is what it seems. Where is the truth?

It is a real comfort to me to know there really is a holy and right standard of truth that cannot be shaken. I know the One who spoke truth, lived truth, and died because of truth, and the One who still lives and speaks the truth. God's ultimate truth remains; man's errant philosophies come and go.

The night before Jesus was tried and crucified, He promised to send us "the Spirit of Truth, whom the world cannot receive, because it neither sees Him nor knows Him; but you know Him, for He dwells with you and will be in you" (John 14:16-17).

This morning, in the book *Inner Chamber* by Andrew Murray, I read a marvelous description of the work of the Holy Spirit:

> It is His ministry to bring the life of God into us, to hide Himself in the depth of our being, and make Himself one with us. There He reveals the Father and Son to be the mighty power of God working in us, taking control of our entire being. He asks only one thing—simple obedience to His leading.[4]

I found once the Holy Spirit came to live in me, Truth came to live there as well. Absolutely honest, totally accurate, completely perfect, intensely alive, never wrong, wise beyond earthly standards, the Spirit is *Truth*.

I discovered this new roommate of mine was kind but not a soft touch, not my buddy pandering to my every desire. He was not like my mother, reminding me of good manners and warning me of danger. Sometimes He drew back from me, expressing His disapproval of my actions, motives, or attitudes. The Spirit often advised me with simple words and then watched to see if I would hear, comprehend, and obey. Because of His presence I had access to wisdom beyond my natural intelligence. How great!

I recognized that unlike self-centered me, the Spirit was totally committed to holiness, righteousness, integrity, honesty, kindness, and mercy. In His presence there is no hedging on the truth, no compromise. God's holiness is the standard. The Spirit is never confused about right and wrong, good and evil, wisdom and foolishness.

I'm thankful He taught me His ways, taking me by the hand, leading me always deeper into the knowledge of God the Father and God the Son.

---

[4] Andrew Murray, *The Inner Chamber* (Fort Washington, Pennsylvania: Christian Literature Crusade, 1981), 113

To be honest, the Spirit's kind of truth, *real* truth, frequently offends me. It is difficult to hear, harder still to absorb, and much harder to apply. The Spirit constantly challenges my statements, stripping away my false presumptions and justifications for little lies by quietly asking,

What did you say? Was it the truth?

With those simple words I stop carelessly saying whatever makes me look important and examine my words. Unfortunately, I often disregard the quiet questions. Instead I go on my merry way, speaking untrue words. By not telling the truth, or not saying the whole of the matter, or exaggerating, or just plain lying, I barricade myself from *real* truth.

I find that my usual way of doing things is easier to maintain while the Spirit's way requires ongoing effort to effect change. The real questions are, Do I really want to change and become honest? Do I love the Truth?

The Holy Spirit doesn't put up with my disregard. He continually confronts me:

Why are you lying? Go back to the person you lied to and confess the lie; tell the truth.

Oh, brother—I surely don't want to do that. I argue, procrastinate, and disobey, but He won't be put off. I finally have to tell the truth and confess my lie. This humbling experience brings change. Mindful of His standard, I learn to stop and think about my own words before I speak.

You would think the Holy Spirit would be satisfied. Nope! Bit by bit He chips away at the root of my dishonesty and reveals deeper and deeper truth about myself. Unfortunately I am resistant to his revelations. Why?

I found the answer in a teaching called "The Arena of Truth" by Bob Mumford. This story perfectly illustrates human resistance to the truth.

The Table Story

Some friends and I had spent several Saturday afternoons building a wooden dining table. After carefully cutting the pieces, we assembled and glued them together, and then sanded the wood until it was satin smooth. Everything looked great. We thought it was ready for the finish. We were so proud—until—another friend who hadn't been involved in the project, came by to see the table. He looked at it from every angle; we waited for his congratulatory praise. He simply said, "It is bowed in the middle."

"That's not true!" I protested.

"Okay," he said, "I'll get a level and we'll know for sure."

"We don't need a level. The table is flat."

I didn't want to know the truth. I wanted him to leave. Besides, no one had asked him for his opinion anyway!

He proceeded to find a level; placed it on the table top. Sure enough the table was bowed.

"The level must be wrong!" I exclaimed.

I couldn't believe my eyes. I stared at my truth-bearing friend, secretly wanting to take the level and hit him over the head with it. (Of course, I knew about killing the prophet instead of believing his word). I was livid.

I sat down; put my head in my hands, heart-sick, all that work for nothing. Oh, to even think of tearing the whole thing apart was too much. "I won't do it," I moaned. "The table is fine just the way it is," I rationalized. "If he had just kept his mouth shut, I would have been happy with the table." Despondent, I couldn't imagine starting over.

However, now I wasn't satisfied with the imperfect table. Venting my frustration, I cursed under my breath. All the while, I knew that the table had to be fixed.

On the next Saturday, we went to work, tore the table apart. We were crabby and short-tempered; it was not a happy affair. After hours of work, finally the table was finished.

Of course I still had work to do. I resented the interference of my friend, the truth-bearer. The Lord asked, *Mumford, how long are you going to pout?* I was steamed. It took me awhile to stop the pity party and get over it.

———

To me this story powerfully illustrates my human capacity for denial and my dislike of correction. Truth is so difficult to receive. The struggle to change directions and fix what is haywire is daunting. God's perfect, holy standard surely eliminates any wiggle room for compromise. For me, it is difficult to see the error of my ways, accept a perfect standard, commit to the work it takes to change, and then continue the frustrating, humbling and never-ending process of transformation.

The Holy Spirit desires that I discover the beauty of a truthful life, a life totally committed to integrity, wisdom, understanding, and honesty. He is dedicated to the process that will change me into a Christ-bearer—one who carries the image of Jesus into everyday life, one who is alive with life from the other realm, a supernatural life of good character. Committed to His agenda, the Spirit won't give up or move away. All my resisting is useless, a complete waste of energy and time.

Oh, dear, change is always in the wind!

Chapter Twelve

Ease

My Yoke Is Easy, My Burden Is Light

Gracious is the Lord, and righteous;
yes, our God is merciful.
The Lord preserves the simple;
I was brought low, and He helped and saved me.
Return to your rest, O my soul,
for the Lord has dealt bountifully with you.
You have delivered my life from death,
my eyes from tears,
and my feet from stumbling and falling.
I will walk before the Lord
in the land of the living.
—Psalm 116:5-9

June 2010—Good morning, Lord. I'm thankful You don't let me run around all stressed. Your word to me this day:

Relax; be at ease while exuberantly pursuing life!

Ease? When I think of ease I imagine a hot summer day; I'm lying in a hammock, listening to the birds, drinking a tall glass of iced tea, and reading a book.

Jesus, I'm sure Your picture of ease is very different from mine. Your loving dependence upon the Father enabled You to accomplish all He asked You to do without rushing, without anxiety. Therefore it must be possible to live, trusting You are in control of even tiny things; there is no need to worry or fret.

This kind of ease does not come naturally. I often run full-speed ahead, revved up and crisis driven. I'm sure this is not pleasing to the Lord. Only the Holy Spirit makes it possible to live life fully engaged and at ease.

Hurry, Hurry, Fret and Worry

I remember one hysterical morning when a silly concern about not getting everything done before the weekend caused me to power up and race around, trying to be superhuman. The whole scene was ridiculous and quite funny.

I awoke with a start. There was so much to do to be ready for some house guests coming for the weekend. Instead of taking a minute to gather my thoughts, relax, and transition from being asleep to being awake, I hopped out of bed, jumped into the shower, and quickly dressed. Edgy, nerves all a-jingle, I mumbled to myself, "Hurry, hurry, you have *soooo* much to do and little time to do it." Usually I'm humming a merry tune; not that morning. I whipped through the morning chores: doing the dishes and cleaning up the kitchen, vacuuming, and planning a couple of dinners for the coming weekend.

Upon completing the household tasks, I left for town, yelling as I went out the door, "Bob, I'm leaving. See ya sometime after five." My thoughts raced through the list of stops: bank, post office, pharmacy, library, gas station, Home Depot, and several grocery stores. Soon my head ached from taut neck muscles. I noticed I was even leaning forward in the car as if that would get me to town faster. Sure, the foot was heavy on the gas pedal!

After far too long I suddenly realized this preposterous behavior and super pressure was self-imposed and completely unnecessary.

There was no reason for any of it—no emergency, no disaster, no rush. In reality, I had plenty of time to get everything done.

My goodness, what had I been thinking? So I stopped the inner message *hurry, hurry* by taking long, deep breaths to ease the anxiety. Slowly my fragmented, agitated thoughts became quiet; my eyes felt heavy. I knew how ridiculous the entire morning had been. I parked the car and put my head back on the headrest; gentling down, I felt the tension lift. The same chores were still ahead, but now I could do them at ease, fully alert to other people and my environment.

I find it so easy to think it is important to pressure, squeeze, and stuff more and more activities, work, and relationships into smaller and smaller increments of time. It seems multitasking is the only way to get enough accomplished. Living on the edge of insanity seems normal; crisis is often my way to thwart boredom. However, this kind of lifestyle is personally very costly. When life has no ease, the body, mind, and spirit become dis-eased—without ease. Burnout results; all kinds of aches and pains, emotional disorders, and fractured relationships can then beset us.

I wrote several years ago in *In The Midst of the Fray*,[5] "the enemy's strategy is to pester and annoy the beloved of God until we give up, too exhausted and disillusioned to care about anything. He runs us in circles, keeping us scurrying from project to project, crisis to crisis . . . destroying God's workers by simply wearing them to a frazzle."

On this particular crazy morning it was a God-thought that dropped into my mind and finally shifted my attention to the Spirit's agenda:

Stop! Calm down. Let Me order your time.

In the quiet of the moment I realized the morning had gone haywire simply because I had failed to interact with the Lord so He could bring His gentling Spirit into my day. My error came

---

[5] Joan B. Weller, *In The Midst of the Fray* (Enumclaw, Wash.: Winepress Publishing, 2003), 132.

from a false assumption that I was in control, that I could actually change circumstances by being uptight, moving faster, and being more efficient. When I included the Lord in my thoughts and inner communion, I was able to settle down and accomplish a great deal.

Ease returned as I repented of my almighty attitude (I can do it all and do it fast). When I let go of my fear of not getting enough done before the weekend, I was able to quit fretting. In fact I sat in the car and laughed at myself. In my mind's eye I saw an old pioneer woman, cursing and muttering, whip in hand, beating a mule hitched to a wagon. I could just hear her yell, "You lazy critter, if you want some supper, you better hurry along and get to gettin'." After a good laugh, my anxiety was gone. I put the car in gear and went about my business, calm and in my right mind.

An inner ease should be the way we live as we go about ordinary life. In the book *The Way of the Heart,* in the section on prayer, Arsenius, a desert father, a reclusive seeker of God, writes

> Silence and solitude must lead to unceasing prayer. To pray always—this is the real purpose of life. The literal translation of the words "pray always" is "come to rest." This rest, however, has little to do with the absence of conflict or pain. It is a rest in God in the midst of a very intense daily struggle.[6]

Lord, I now know failure to turn to You led to my misery. Independent and disregarding Your counsel, I was sure if I worked fast and hard enough I could accomplish the tasks at hand. If I had started the day asking for help, You would have given me a peaceful confidence, ordering my day, and keeping me in wholesome ease.

---

[6] Henri Nouwen, *The Way of the Heart/Desert Spirituality and Contemporary Ministry* (San Francisco: HarperCollins, 1991), 69.

At the end of the day I would have had a sense of accomplishment and been less tired.

> What I'm trying to do here is get you to relax, not be so preoccupied with *getting* so you can respond to God's *giving*. People who don't know God and the way he works fuss over these things, but you know both God and how he works. Steep yourself in God-reality, God-initiative, God-provisions. You'll find all your everyday human concerns will be met. Don't be afraid of missing out. You're my dearest friends! The Father wants to give you the very kingdom itself (Luke 12:31–32, *The Message*).

O Lord, help me enter into Your rest, trusting You are with me to restore, redeem, and encourage.

Chapter Thirteen

Come!
Gracious Invitation

Jesus cries out, "Come to me, all you who labor and
are heavy laden, and I will give you rest."
—Matthew 11:28

July 2010—Although I find it easy to slip into a deadly routine that destroys my sense of purpose until boredom captures my mind and flab destroys my body, living in intense quietness is the opposite of this. Intense quietness is a way of embracing life with anticipatory excitement, seeing and hearing things beyond the ordinary, God-things: unexpected gifts, delightful conversations, hope in the face of difficulty, provision when there is no money.

It is impossible to enter this place of intense responsiveness to God without hearing and obeying His command, "Come! Come to Me. Come and listen. Come and learn. Come and obey. *Come!*"

Unfortunately, the Lord's invitations are often disregarded. His great *chesed* (mercy, kindness, compassionate love) is rarely received. When Isaiah the prophet wrote that the Messiah would be a man of sorrows and acquainted with grief, I think he was speaking of this very thing—the utter disrespect and rejection of God's invitation, *Come here!*

O Lord, forgive me for being too distracted to even hear Your gracious invitation. Draw me into Your presence that I might experience life filled with Your revelation and counsel. Each day may I pay attention to Your loving invitation so I might know You and receive Your love.

The Come lesson—Oh, yes! God uses many ways to teach us. I learned much about God's imperative "Come!" as I attempted to train a much-neglected golden retriever. He was three years old when he came to live with us, and he would not come on command. Not far into his training I realized this lesson was for me, not the dog. I was the one who wandered off, fiddled around, and wouldn't come when the Lord said, "Come here!"

A number of months after the death of our dog Triple Gold, I asked the Lord, "Can we have another dog?" The answer came a few days later when we were given another golden. On our first meeting this happy, big, beautiful fellow with white fringes and silky blond fur enthusiastically greeted us with little jumps and a wagging tail. A city dog, confined to a small apartment, he had never been free to roam, hunt, dig, or swim. He was in for a crash course in country living.

We brought him home to our unfenced ten acres, called him Copper, and laughed at his antics. Being familiar with the cacophony of the city, he was startled at the hooting owls, yapping coyotes, and croaking frogs. To keep him from barking at every little sound during the night, we left a radio on for a few weeks. Accustomed to walking only on sidewalks and mowed lawns, he refused to investigate the tall grass or wander into the forest.

Copper was immediately responsive to Bob, constantly bringing him things and nipping at his gloved hands. However, to my dismay he was aloof and unresponsive to me. In fact he would jump back every time I tried to touch him.

When released from the leash, he stayed close, playing keep-away, chase me, and run-around, but he would not come. Obedience to the simple commands of come, sit, no, and stay was a must for his safety. I began his training, and in the process I learned many lessons as well.

———

August 2001—Lord, I'm close to tears. I'm so disappointed. Copper doesn't come, and he won't retrieve worth a nickel. He won't bring me anything.

Surprises always involve relinquishment.
Relinquish what?

Your disappointment.
Your expectations.

Enjoy what is.
Be creatively patient yet firm.
Let him come to you when he is ready.

Oh, brother, that will never happen.

———

September—progress! I had the sweetest time with Copper today. He was lying on his side on the rug in the house, playing with his ball. I got on the floor, lying on my side and facing him. With several light touches I tapped his paws with my hand. He stopped playing. I waited for several seconds. While still lying on his side, with tongue hanging out and a little sparkle in his eye, he batted the ball to me with the back of his paw. I held it for a few seconds, and then rolled it back to him. Back and forth it went. There were several long pauses—wait, wait, wait, the waiting game—and then he sent it back. He was *mine* for these few minutes. So great! Maybe I can establish a bond with him, an invisible bond of devotion.

———

Lord, thanks for caring about little things like giving us another dog. Help me be patient with him as he learns to come on command.

———

November—Copper is still on the lead and won't be released until he obeys. Even in the house he just looks at me, wags his tail, but won't come. He is learning manners and some commands; however, he loves to tease, staying just out of reach, deliberately disobeying.

———

He is perfect for you.
Open your heart and love him.

Watch him and notice his signals.
Touch him.
Encourage him when he does something right.
Retrain what has been neglected.

Lord, these words of Yours apply to many relationships, don't they? Help me see how You draw us into relationship with You. Show me how You build invisible love-bonds with Your followers.

———

January—Some freedom! I think Copper is ready for a little freedom. I'll take him up on the canyon trail and turn him loose. I think he'll stay close to me. It will be a challenge to catch him and put him on lead before we start for home, but it's worth a try.

Oh, he had such fun, rolling around on the creek bank until he rolled right off, tumbling into the water upside down. Sprinting out of the water, shaking, turning in circles like a tornado, he was all joy. I laughed and laughed.

February—A red-letter day! Copper came on command. So great! We were coming home from a long hike; I needed to put him on lead before getting to the main road. I stopped in the middle of the trail; I turned to face him and stood absolutely still. Trailing behind me about thirty feet, he stopped and looked at me. "Copper, come!" I yelled. He cocked his ears. I repeated the command and hand signal. He tilted his head to the side, then—very, very, very slowly crept a few steps closer, then stopped. I waited, one minute, then another, then another. It seemed like forever. He edged a bit closer and stopped twenty feet away. Holding my breath, I stood still—waiting, waiting, waiting—the waiting game. Suddenly, he bolted, running straight toward me. At the last minute he gave a little joy hop and sat at my feet. "Yes!" We danced round and round in celebration and then headed home.

Oh, yes! Great Patient One, You celebrate with us when we *get it!*

March—Joy. Today I took Copper to the big pond on the bamboo farm. I threw a stick into the water; when I released him from the lead, he plunged into the water, got the stick, and immediately brought it back, dropping it at pond's edge, and then sat waiting for me to throw it again. My goodness, he loves retrieving from the water. How great! After an hour of this it was time to go. Needing to put him back on lead, I whistled for him. Instead of coming, he had a joy attack, racing around and around in circles, running full speed ahead, straight toward me. At the last second he jived to the side, just brushing my leg and circling around again, speeding past. Around and around he went, just barely brushing by as he ran at full tilt. Finally he stopped and barked, then raced up to me, shaking vigorously, getting me soaking wet, and sat down right in front of me. What fun!

July—Obedience leads to freedom. I'm so happy when Copper obeys because I know obedience leads to freedom and joy. My big yeller dog is making progress. Does he come? Sometimes, when he wants to, when it's convenient, when he's finished with his swimming, digging, or chasing deer.

———

Hmmmm—Sounds like me. I absolutely know when I come at Your command, Lord, I get to participate in great and mighty God-things. Yet my old nature always wants to procrastinate, or argue, or do my own thing. I'm so sorry. I wonder what adventures I've missed because of my fiddling around.

———

The Copper adventures and training continued for two more years. Then it was over.

April—Easter Week—Copper is very sick. The veterinarian gives us terrible news. "Copper is bleeding into his belly from a cancerous tumor in his spleen. There is nothing we can do."

So my big golden boy is no more. We bury him at the base of a huge Douglas fir. Bleeding hearts, Johnny-jump-ups, and trillium grace his grave.

———

Easter Morning—Thanks, Lord, for Copper. Tears come each time I remember the gentle giant of a dog. My heart grieves; my spirit knows how much You desire to give us life and how awful death is—even for a dog. You give and You take away, but everything, our rejoicing as well as our sorrow, is Your gift.

———

The sun peeks out on this Easter Day. We are blessed with the Lord's presence. Even though it seems impossible, I know my heart will heal and be able to embrace another hiking buddy—another faithful, responsive dog friend who loves the adventure of hikes in the canyon country and is my companion on night walks. Right now the intimacy of darkness is too empty to endure. It brings back memories of other times, of desperate loneliness when death crowded in to tear the heart, rip the soul, sicken the body. Tonight I can't walk in the moonlight. Copper is not with me to alert to danger, to help me listen to the night sounds. I'm blind and deaf.

Yet I know grief enlarges my heart, and I'm incredibly grateful. A miracle occurs; hope hovers near. At some point the tide turns, sorrow dissipates. Life beyond loss begins once more.

———

Thanks, Father, for Jesus, the One who always came to You, listening, responding, and embracing everything You planned for Him. You were greatly pleased. May I build an invisible love tie to You, constantly listening to Your voice and obeying Your Word. What a miracle that would be.

Chapter Fourteen

The Gleaner
Obtaining Spiritual Food

So she gleaned in the field until evening.
—Ruth 2:17

August 2010—Wow! Yesterday, as we drove toward town, a huge red-tailed hawk swooped down ten feet in front of the car, picked up a rat on the pavement, and flew off with its prey to a nearby tree. It was so great! What a show to see the raptor at work!

———

Lord, this morning, I'm so grateful You have opened my eyes and my ears, enabling me to recognize Your presence and understand some of Your words. What a gracious gift! It is so wonderful to enjoy Your provision, the spiritual insights and written Word given to me by Your Holy Spirit. I remember what You said several years ago about the Scripture.

As you read Scripture, ask me about what you read. I will give you treasure hidden under the surface of the words. As I accomplish quietness in you, you will be able to see beyond the words into life.

Lose nothing I give you. Write down the nuggets of truth, capturing the essence of life-giving. When you share these insights with others, they will be encouraged, strengthened, and enlightened.

It takes some discipline, focus, and time to see beyond the obvious storyline and into the real essence of Scripture. When I began reading the Word, I was spiritually blind. However, somewhere down the line I became aware that the surface truths are the "outward and visible signs of inward and spiritual grace." They are sacramental. The Author of the words, the Lord, is mysteriously infused in the text of Scripture.

Quite astonishingly I found the search for spiritual food is not primarily about finding things. It's not an intellectual pursuit; it's not about obtaining truth or answers to problems or peace or comfort, as desirable as these are. It's about knowing the Lord. Unless my search leads to communion with Him, I'm just looking for information. The Holy Spirit, who is present all the time, waits silently for an invitation to explain the written Word to me. The real Treasure, the Translator between the kingdom of God and the things of earth, is with me. When I ask Him to answer my questions, He opens my spiritual eyes and ears, and sometimes I actually understand the Scriptures better; details and context, insight and directives become mine.

Let me be clear: spiritual food comes from the Spirit of God infusing the written Word with meaning and application. Without Him, it is easy to miss the richness contained in Scripture. When Jesus told a story, almost everyone could actually understand and enjoy it. However, a few curious ones asked Him to explain what He was *really* saying. He then opened revelation, using words pregnant with meaning, filled with life. Each word contained things not seen but real and powerful nonetheless.

When the Spirit of God enlightens the mysteries hidden in the Words of Scripture and shares them with believers, divine communion takes place. Receiving His kind of wondrous, spiritual provision is exciting because it is not a thing at all—it is God Himself.

Hearing the Word in depth is a matter of the heart—not complicated or weird but simple and straightforward. When I realize the Spirit is with me, my reading of the Word slows way down. I stop and talk with Him about what I read and then listen for His instruction. I must be thorough in my study: hearing, understanding, obeying, and living a few Words instead of whipping through oceans of words and not heeding any of them. I receive nothing of value when I'm distracted or hurried.

I often think of myself as a gleaner, gathering nuggets of truth others drop, finding grain growing in weeds. I treasure Truth overlooked and left behind. This God-food sometimes seems sparse, yet it sustains me for years. When shared with others, these miraculous kernels of truth nourish them as well. Constantly amazed by the surprises I find, my heart overflows with gratefulness.

A gleaner is not a laborer working for a paycheck. The desperate poor are the ones who glean. They must find food or starve. The gleanings are life-giving and precious, the work continuous, the hunger unrelenting. However, if the gleaner knows God is the source of spiritual food, then everything he or she finds is a gift, a sign of grace.

The Old Testament Book of Ruth contains a vivid picture of a gleaner. Loyal, loving, diligent, and obedient, Ruth gleaned wheat and barley in the fields and then shared what she had gathered with her elderly mother-in-law. Into this simple picture comes Boaz, the kinsman redeemer, a perfect type of Jesus. Oh, yes, the story of Ruth is not just about finding wheat; it's about knowing God, who protects, provides, covers, respects, and restores not only Ruth but also Naomi and Boaz.

———

My Great Friend, I'm astonished at what You show me in Your Word. O Jesus, Son of David, help me find the real Treasure!

Chapter Fifteen

Follow Me
The Way to the Father

Whoever desires to come after Me, let him deny
himself, and take up his cross, and follow Me.
—Mark 8:34-38

August 2010—As I begin this entry in my journal I feel sort
of sad and nostalgic, longing for friends and family no longer
in my life. I realize this sorrow is normal, not unusual but one
strand in my life's tapestry. There are other strands: memories of
marvelous adventures, great conversations, and family gatherings;
there are times of sickness and injury, joy and tenderness, anger
and disappointment. The Lord weaves them all into a beautiful,
grace-filled tapestry—a masterpiece.

———

Lord, I'm so thankful You have been with our family through
this difficult year. We are coming up to the anniversary of Adam's
death. For Molly and Don, grief has overshadowed their days, tears
come easily; anger and frustration often rise to the surface. The
finality of death has settled in—their son is gone. Only memories
remain. It takes courage and tenacity for them to keep doing
ordinary family things, loving and caring for their remaining
children.

Meditation on Mark 10:32-33

August 22, 2010—As I read the Gospel of Mark this morning I particularly noticed this verse: "Now they were on the road, going up to Jerusalem, and Jesus was going before them; and they were bewildered and as they followed they were seized with fear" (Mark 10:32).

Up to this point the disciples had watched Jesus perform miracles and explain the things of the kingdom of God. They must have been thrilled by the spectacular, miraculous drama unfolding before their eyes.

Suddenly the emphasis changed, the message shifted. Jesus told them, "Behold, we are going up to Jerusalem, and the Son of Man will be turned over to the chief priests and the scribes; and they will condemn and sentence Him to death and turn Him over to the Gentiles. And they will mock Him and spit on Him, and whip Him and put Him to death; but after three days He will rise again" (Mark 10:33).

The disciples didn't understand. They argued, "No, this will not happen to You!" They vowed, "We'll be there even if it costs our lives." They asked, "Who will be the greatest in Your kingdom?" Philip wanted more evidence in order to convince himself of God's presence. Murderous Judas counted the bag money. The Lord alone knew the full implications of the assignment ahead; the disciples just didn't get it.

Walking alone toward terrible and sorrowful things, Father-things, Jesus left the intimate fellowship with His disciples and headed toward Jerusalem, the Passover, the New Covenant, and death. Following at a distance, the disciples trudged along behind, no longer enthused. Jesus motioned, *Come. Follow Me!*

The Jerusalem Journey

If I project myself into the story, there is no way I would have gone to Jerusalem. I would have wanted this wonderful man to just be my friend, or shepherd, or companion, or rabbi, but not to die. "No, no, no way!" I would have wailed, "I need You; the people need You; You can't just go to Jerusalem and quit." I would have pleaded with Him, sobbing and weeping, "I don't understand!"

He would have kindly answered, "I know."

Jesus wanted to take me to His places, but I wouldn't have gone. Terribly afraid, I would have known the Jerusalem journey would be rough, the way obscure, the end frightful. The Lord would have beckoned, *Come. Follow Me! I'm going to the Father. You will see His magnificent love.*

In Jerusalem Jesus was rejected, betrayed, beaten, falsely accused, tortured, and crucified. It is impossible to even imagine such suffering. The ugliness of the cross and the anguish of the beloved Son are beyond human understanding.

If I didn't know the end of the story, I would think the Father's love was ugly and tormenting. I would ask, "How could a loving Father allow such pain, such wickedness, such depravity to fall on His Son?" I would never have conceived of such a thing. It would be too judgmental, too final, and too harsh.

Father, Your love goes beyond the human framework, off the page, out of time and our reality. Your love involves giving up life so many can live. It involves obedience without reserve. It demands exclusivity and passion. Your love is filled with sorrow yet overflowing with hope. Your love places upon the beloved Son evil, hatred, sickness, hunger, rebellion, and death.

During the desperate hours the Son suffered, Father, You hovered close. The cost of redemption to the Son and to You was unfathomable. Yet the Son's obedience brought You great joy. After Jesus was dead, You had Him gently placed into the earth, the holy precious Seed buried, waiting. Father, You knew through death life springs forth—copious, wondrous, and glorious life from the eternal realm.

As I contemplate these mysteries, I am deeply convicted of my self-focus. The Jerusalem walk requires a complete abandonment to the Father and what He wants to accomplish. Turning my back on Jerusalem, I can often be found by the fire of my own making, praying Jesus will come and make me happy.

My love for the Lord is often determined by how I feel. I want Him to heal me so I will not suffer. I ask Him questions so I will be smarter. I work hard to be a better person so I will be loved. My love for the Lord is about me. Oh, dear! It is all about *me*, not the Lord, not the Father!

O Lord, help me. I want to follow You; the road to Jerusalem leads to the only life there is. I need Your Holy Spirit to pull me along, release me from passivity and selfishness, and push me from behind when I want to sit down. When I'm discouraged and dismayed, help me welcome Your painful way of bringing me into the Father's glorious presence.

When I recognize that no human can fill the loneliness and my need for love, the Holy Spirit tenderly heals my wounds, my sorrow, my loneliness, my longing for comfort, filling the emptiness in my heart with resurrection life, His life. This kind of life comes after death; it is the fruit of suffering.

Jesus, the Great Redeemer, walked through rejection, betrayal, torture, and sin-bearing. Moving deeper into the darkness of death, He motions, *Come! Follow Me! The things you think are important and the pursuit of them, take life from you. Follow Me though suffering and death. True treasure is ahead. Your tears of sorrow will be changed to weeping-joy and whirling-dance.*

Part IV

Intimacy

My dear journey mate,

We are well along on our journey. I hope you have been deeply touched by the Spirit.

In intense quietness God draws close. Conversation with Him is a continuous listening, hearing, responding, loving, and knowing. Relationship deepens; friendship turns to love. Listening to the Beloved is wonderful. Being with Him is life itself.

Chapter Sixteen

Struggle
Questions, Questions, Questions

Hear, O Israel, the Lord our God, the Lord is one.
And you shall love the Lord your God with all your
heart, with all your soul, with all your mind, and with
all your strength.

—Mark 12:30

October 2010—By now I should know what it means to love
the Lord with my whole heart, soul, mind, and strength, yet I still
question: is it actually possible? How? What would wholehearted
love be like?

As I thought about love and friendship, I realized any intimate
relationship starts with great respect and honor of another person.
There has to be a freedom to tell it like it is without the fear of
rejection, betrayal, or disregard. Deeply held ideas and feelings
can be shared in ordinary conversation. Each person must be
responsive to the other, caring for the other's insights, stories, and
needs. Life is shared, the dark times of grief and stress as well as
times of delight and fun, laughter and joy. There comes a peaceful
rhythm between expressions of love and tenderness, between
silence and solitude. As the years go by, the *knowing* of each other
deepens. There is compassionate love, physical closeness, and
emotional equality.

———

So, Jesus, is it possible to love You more and more, deeper and deeper? My life itself is a gift from You, so how can I give You anything? My love is shallow and contained, flawed and tiny compared to Your constant, compassionate loving-kindness and overflowing mercy. You are so good, so magnificent (so unlike me) that all I can do is stand amazed and worship You, living God.

———

Sadly enough and quite honestly, I often put off being with the Lord. Many of my interests are earthly, having little to do with spiritual matters. Just as I finally get quiet, desiring communion with the Lord, something else in me wants to get up and do this or that. Then all my talk about intense quietness seems a sham, my lack of consistency becoming terribly clear.

Many times instead of being able to sense the presence of Jesus I catch only glimpses, hear pieces of His Word, feel touches of divine presence; focus is rare. I hear the Word mixed with my own thoughts. I see so imperfectly that it is like peering through fog, the vision muddled and indistinct. However, under all this confusion I deeply know there is another reality—the way life should be.

———

Is it possible to be aware of Your presence at all times? I want to know You and be in love with You as a bride loves the bridegroom: seeing, hearing, smelling, and touching him—human realities. Can I be in constant companionship with You as a bride on her honeymoon?

Do you want an answer?

Yes!

My dear little friend, if you believe I Am [alive, present, active, and strong], *then every moment of your life will be filled with awareness of My presence. You live in the dimension of time, and your life is a series of many, many little moments, tasks, thoughts, and experiences. I'm always present.*

As you expect to see Me in your ordinary life, My love, thoughts, and direction will be opened to you. Knowing Me comes from catching the action—the watching. You then learn who I am, what I do, and My desires. The surprising interdictions, the supernatural God-encounters, the bursts of insight, and the desire to love me are My way of helping you come to know Me.

You say you want to love Me. Where do you think love comes from? Only the Spirit of God can give you the desire to love and be loved. The Spirit is close, so close that you think this love originates with you. It does not. It comes from Me. I indwell you. As I love the Father, as I love you, as I love people, you get to participate in that love. In essence, hearing My words or seeing My actions, or participating in My passion, or sharing My thoughts results in continuous revelation. You therefore know me with increasing appreciation and wonder. Because you love Me, you will know the Father and love Him. During every moment of your day My Spirit reveals My presence and the Father's love. The Spirit actively directs your thoughts, delights in you, and brings life out of death.

You naturally respond with thanksgiving and joy. You see the wondrous glory in created nature and rejoice. You hear praise and enter in. You love everything I give you, and you are thankful. You often awaken with songs of love and praise; I love your singing and your passion. You share with others what is real, what you have seen, what you have touched. Deep and intimate love for others is the outflow of My love for you.

"When I consider Your heavens, the work of Your fingers, the moon and the stars, which You have ordained, what is man that You are mindful of him, the son of man that You visit him?"

(Psalm 8:3-4).

Your love, Lord, is without limits and marvelous. I'm silent before you!

Chapter Seventeen

Indwelling

Christ in You, the Hope of Glory

To them God willed to make known what are
the riches of the glory of this mystery among the
Gentiles: which is Christ in you the hope of glory.
—Colossians 1:27

November 5, 2010—I'm thankful for a couple of warm, sunny days after the chilly rain. Yesterday was absolutely beautiful, the fall color show spectacular. The blueberry bushes, growing in our little valley, have turned bright red. The brilliant yellow, orange, and purple of the deciduous trees stand in contrast to the dark green of the firs and cedars. Geese and ducks fly over in long, trailing, arrow patterns. Red-and-yellow, white-and-brown mushrooms dot the forest floor. Whirling leaves, maple helicopter seeds, and fir needles fly across the sky set free by a cold east wind. Yes indeed, our place is a glorious mess. Bob will be blowing leaves off the roof and lawn for hours.

Thanks, Lord, for the change in seasons, for the beauty all around us, and most especially for Your constant presence, Your indwelling in my heart and life.

The other day I was reading along in the New Testament book of Colossians, not especially paying very much attention to what I was reading. Suddenly I noted a familiar phrase: "Christ in you, the hope of glory." At first I thought I knew what the words meant, but then I realized if I had to explain the meaning to anyone else I would be hard-pressed to do so.

"Christ in you, the hope of glory"—Hmmm.

I slowly reread chapter one of Paul's epistle, an amazing and magnificent statement of the centrality of the Christ. "We look at this Son and see the God who cannot be seen. We look at this Son and see God's original purpose in everything created. For everything, absolutely everything, above and below, visible and invisible . . . everything got started in him and finds its purpose in him. He was there before any of it came into existence and holds it all together right up to this moment" (Colossians 1:15-17, *The Message*).

Then Paul states, "to them God willed to make known what are the riches of glory of this mystery among the Gentiles: which is Christ in you the hope of glory" (Colossians 1:27, *The Message*). *Mystery* and *glory* occurring together—I had no idea what either meant in the context of this Scripture. So began my treasure hunt, one that deeply affected my life.

Word Meanings

Mystery in this scripture means truth already exists but cannot be apprehended until God reveals it. The mystery is the revelation of Jesus the Christ, His life, death, resurrection, and then His indwelling of His followers by the Holy Spirit. Paul's teaching revealed to the church this previously hidden truth of Jesus, the Messiah.

To me, *glory* had always been a bright, luminous splendor described in the Old Testament as "the glory of the Lord filled the temple," a sign of God's presence.

Webster's dictionary defines *glory* as bestowing honor, praise, admiration. A glorious thing or person is magnificent, majestic, perfect, delightful, wonderful, splendid, lustrous, and renowned. To give glory means to praise, honor, worship, thank, and exalt.[7]

Glory in this scripture seemed to mean something entirely different. As I thought about this I remembered Moses' request of God, "Please, show me Your glory" (Exodus 33:18). In reply God cautioned,

> I will make all my goodness pass before you, and I will proclaim the name of the Lord before you . . . You cannot see My face; for no man shall see Me, and live . . . Here is a place by Me, and you shall stand on the rock. So it shall be, while My glory passes by, that I will put you in the cleft of the rock, and will cover you with My hand while I pass by, then I will take away My hand, and you shall see My back; but My face shall not be seen. (Exodus 33:18-23)

> Then the Lord came down covering Moses with His hand and proclaimed, "The Lord, the Lord God, merciful and gracious, long-suffering, and abounding in goodness and truth, keeping mercy for thousands, forgiving iniquity and transgression, and sin, by no means clearing the guilty." (Exodus 34:6-7)

I realized that here was God introducing Himself. "I Am, I Am God merciful, gracious, long-suffering, abounding in goodness and truth, forgiving, and just."

Suddenly it dawned on me. God's glory is His goodness.

"Christ in you, the hope of glory" seemed to mean Jesus takes up permanent residence in believers, bringing His glory, His goodness. This magnificent experience is truly incredible and absolutely astonishing. Because of the Lord's intimate presence in

---

[7] *Webster's   Ninth   New   Collegiate   Dictionary* (Springfield,   Mass.: Merriam-Webster, 1984).

my house, everything is affected: my thoughts, my behavior, my decisions, and my desires, to name just a few.

———

Honored Guest, I'm delighted to have You in my home. You are so gracious; in fact, Your name should be Grace, except that seems to be a girl's name. No matter—You are grace incarnate. It is impossible to appreciate You and serve You enough, My King.

It is unbelievable that You enjoy being with me. As I chatter along, You listen with delight at my adventures, hear my prayers, and enjoy my constant inquiries. I feel understood and affirmed even when I feel sorry for myself or complain. Tenderly commiserating with my concerns, You often laugh at my ridiculous fears, knowing I have nothing to worry about since You are with me. Before I know anything is wrong, You know my need. When You speak truth to me, my perspective changes, anxiety dissipates, despair stops. I'm forgiven and healed because of Your merciful presence. I enjoy peace, a God-peace. I can rest.

How great! Thank you so much my wonderful Savior, my Jesus.

However, I found You are not just an appreciative guest in my home but You are Lord, all powerful, all knowing, and perfect. In Your presence it takes only a second for me to sense Your authority. Holy is present. Holy, holy . . . You are holy! I am awestruck, afraid, and at the same time wonder-filled.

My world shifts from comparing myself with others to knowing real perfection, complete wholeness. I am sinful and broken. I want to collapse in terror and conviction. There is no pretending to be good; You are good, and I am just trying to be good. I expect harsh criticism, but instead I hear *Come, come, and learn of me, for I am lowly and meek of heart.* Loving, compassionate Savior, You show me the way to change, one step, then another, then another. As I obey, You see my efforts and forgive my blunders. Mercy covers me. Truth touches my illusions and changes them into God-desire.

Quite miraculously there are times when I realize Your glory, Your goodness flows from me to others. You initiate this phenomenon. I sense Your presence and hear a whispered instruction: insight into Scripture, understanding of a particular circumstance, or supernatural knowledge about a person. Usually this kind of knowing needs explanation. I ask, "Lord, what is this about, and what am I to do?"

I wait, alert for the answer. Sometimes You say, *Pray*. Other times I run into someone and immediately know it is a divine appointment. As I pray for the person or situation, my soul with all its criticism and judgment seems to withdraw, making my thoughts of no consequence. Then my spirit, full of Your love, rises and is empowered by Your Spirit. It is as if a door opens inside me; You flow through my feeble mind, emotions, and intuition ministering wisdom, comfort, forgiveness, and love. Healing takes place, sin is revealed and confessed, peace replaces confusion, hope springs out of despair, Your mercy covers shame, and the person or situation changes forever.

During this encounter, feeling Your passion for the one in need, I am overwhelmed by Your love. Your power flows over my meager emotional system. I'm undone yet fully aware that the miraculous has happened. I get the great privilege of participating in an eternal event. I'm filled with adoration.

Intimacy with the indwelling Lord is beyond words, beyond thought, beyond human love.

Chapter Eighteen

Spiritual Hunger
Longing and Loneliness

He awakens me morning by morning,
He awakens my ear
To hear as the learned.
—Isaiah 50:4

Winter begins today. I'm glad because now the days begin to get longer, and before you know it spring is here. The rainy season is a great time for me to quiet down and think about my inner life.

Lord, it is only as I gain some stillness inside that I experience intimacy with You. In the quiet place I anticipate seeing wondrous things of creation; I recall insights and revelation of who You are and what You have done and are doing; my thoughts and ideas take on a direction and purpose; I'm comforted and secure; fear ends.

In *Subversive Spirituality* by Eugene Peterson, there is a wonderful description of being in the Lord's presence:

> When we enter into the Lord's presence, we find a place of adoration and listening. This allows an infusion of God-energy that comes and releases obedience. God speaks; things happen. We understand who we are and where we are; who God is and where He is. It is a place of intense focus that gathers and concentrates energy that on signal from God's imperative (go, come,

listen) expresses itself in precise obedience—running in the way of God's commandments. It is a place to which we return so that our faith is God-initiated, our discipleship is Christ-defined, and our obedience is spirit-infused. We must return to this quiet place to listen and change. He always takes us to Jerusalem and the cross and resurrection. We adore and we listen.[8]

Listening to the Lord sometimes is beyond my ability; it is hard to become quiet inside and then expectant. I desire so much to know the Lord in a deeper and a more intimate way and to personally hear the Words of Scripture. It is imperative that I not only sit down and wait but also become quiet in thought and emotion.

At first, when I try to become tuned in to the Spirit I find my thoughts scattered; I'm concerned about this and that, mere minutiae. But if I wait quietly and listen, there comes a time when I begin to perceive things at a deeper level. I see my fear of many things, my judgment of others, my self-centeredness. Little imaginary dramas start playing out in my mind, the "what ifs," "should haves," and "if only" scenarios. If I am impatient and condemning with this disquiet, I become entrapped in these surface thoughts and never reach quietness.

However, if I wait and listen, I discover that underneath all this humanness is another whole area where there is a yearning, a longing for comfort and love. Intimacy with God starts here; *the longing, the loneliness, is really a hunger for the Lord.*

The temptation is to try to relieve this empty feeling with substitutes: a change in environment, someone to talk with, a candy bar, or a little entertainment.

It is imperative that I remember: *this yearning is God-hunger, satisfied only by being with the Lord.*

---

8   Eugene Peterson, *Subversive Spirituality* (Vancouver, B.C.: William B. Eerdmans Publishing, Regent College Publishing, 1997), 28, 29.

This longing is a God-given gift of indescribable value. David expressed his hunger for the Lord in Psalm 42: "As the deer pants for the water brooks, so my soul longs for You, O God; My soul thirsts for God, for the Living God." In David's youthful years shepherding was a lonely, quiet affair; he had time to listen and hear the God of Israel. As his life became more complicated with warfare and kingship, David longed for times alone with the Lord, the God of Israel. Many of David's psalms express this God-hunger.

Jesus, like David, also loved being with Father God away from the pressing crowds of people. Out of his constant communion with the Father came the authority to speak words of great wisdom: "The Lord God has given Me the tongue of the learned, that I should know how to speak a word in season to him who is weary. He awakens Me morning by morning, He awakens My ear; and I was not rebellious, nor did I turn away" (Isaiah 50:4-5).

Jesus spoke of His absolute communion with His Father: "I and the Father are one" (John 10:30). "I am One who bears witness of Myself, and the Father who sent Me bears witness of Me" (John 8:18). "When you lift up the Son of Man, then you will know that I am He, and that I do nothing of Myself; but as My Father taught Me, I speak these things. And He who sent Me is with Me. The Father has not left Me alone, for I always do those things that please Him" (John 8:28-29). "He who has seen Me has seen the Father" (John 14:9).

I wondered what Jesus' communion with the Father was like? How did He pray? Could He have used the Book of Psalms as a prayer book? It was the prayer book and hymnal of the Jewish people. I tried an experiment. Using my imagination, I took some of the words of David in Psalm 42 and wrote a prayer in which Jesus talks with His Father. (The resulting prayer is not meant to be scripturally correct but an inspirational and personal meditation.) My goodness, what a surprise; by writing this psalm in this way, I was privileged to sense the communion between Jesus and the Father.

Jesus Prays Psalm 42

I hunger for You, Father. In this dry, barren place, I am like a deer in the wilderness who finds a deep ravine, shaded and cool, with water bubbling up from a hidden river deep under the desert. I find You, My Father. You refresh me, You My Source, You, the Ever-Present One. Renewing strength comes from our fellowship, the love We share, that enduring love that always has been, that love that welcomes, that rejoices, that enjoys communion together. Father, You alone satisfy the longing of My heart.

As I walk the corrupted earth, I am a man of sorrows and acquainted with grief. I came to reveal You, Father, but many are blind and deaf. My beloved friends live doubting that You are present, that We love the ones We have created. How can it be that people remain unaware of Your wondrous presence? My tears are for them. Even a touch of their separation, isolation, or emptiness causes agony in me. I run to You, My Father.

For all eternity We have exchanged life together: We love, We speak words filled with creative, abounding life. We listen as the words burst forth and produce life, and then together We behold the wonder of what We create. We love and adore, dancing and singing. The water of the desert now springs forth from within, pouring out in thanksgiving and celebration.

As I walk the earth, My soul often becomes overwhelmed by sadness. However, Father, You are not cast down. As I'm with You, My sorrow evaporates like the morning mist. I'm praising and adoring You. Memories flood into My spirit, and I repeat them to You. Sometimes man's blindness and preoccupations threaten to crush Me like rapids in a river or waves crashing upon a beach, but then I'm immersed in Your love. Your songs cover me in the night. Father, You are life itself; Your presence is My prayer.

I struggle. There is no relief from the scorning attack designed to kill me. "If You are the Son of God, prove it." "If God is so great, where is He?" I *am* with them day and night, yet they cannot perceive My presence. Then I draw close to You, beholding You, My Father, Source of life.

In this meditation Word and Spirit came together. I was immersed in eternal life. The Father was close; Jesus was intimately present; the Spirit lived in these words. No matter how often I reread these words I'm always transported into communion with the Lord. This truly is a place of listening and adoration. My spirit rests in the Lord's great love. My hunger increases; I love this interchange, this quietness, this rest. A deep stillness touches my thoughts. His comfort surrounds me.

O Lord, how I long to experience Your presence, Your constant teaching and fellowship. I'm always on the alert to hear Your voice or sense Your love or hear Your truth. Nothing satisfies this fire You have lit within me except when I'm aware of Your presence. I'm ruined! I live to hear Your Word, understand Your heart, love as you do, and live in the secret place of the Most High.

Chapter Nineteen

Shepherd Chasing
Leaving Home

The Lord is my shepherd, I shall not want.
—Psalm 23:1

Throughout the Old and New Testaments the language is often poetic; many metaphors create pictures—the Lord, a shepherd who cares for His sheep. One day as I was thinking about God's extraordinary love, I imagined being a little lamb, following the Good Shepherd up into the mountains. My imaginary journey that morning brought me into a beautiful experience with the Lord.

The Little Lamb and the Shepherd

I'm sound asleep in the sheepfold.
Come on, get up, it's time to go.
Rousted out of my warm bed among the others, I run after the Shepherd who is far ahead. "Wait, wait—I'm coming." He doesn't answer but keeps to a brisk pace up the path leading into the mountains.

I've never left the fenced field before or been separated from the other sheep. I'm a little scared; the terrain is steep. I catch up with my Shepherd and keep right behind Him.

"Where are we going?" I ask. Catching a little nibble of the sweet grass growing beside the trail, I wonder why I'm here and not with the others in the sheepfold. We continue up the steep trail into the mountains until finally we enter an open meadow, a hidden valley; the grass is lush, I eat and am satisfied. I drink from a quiet running stream. Spring flowers are everywhere.

My Shepherd sits down and calls me to His side.

Come, my beloved!

I'm amazed by His love and tenderness. We rest. At long last, distracted no more I listen and learn, taking in His life-giving words.

I'm so glad you heard My voice and came with Me today, my little friend. I call for my sheep, but often they are too busy looking for food and water in the sheepfold to hear my call. They find cut hay, feed from the feed bag, and drink stale water from the trough. The caretakers do not risk taking the sheep to the high country. "It's too dangerous; with no fences, the sheep scatter. Besides, the sheep need routine. It's easier for us to keep them safe and secure in the pen. The big dog guards the fence line so we can leave them."

My plan is very different. Sheep are dependent critters. I love the sheep and long to take them to hidden valleys filled with abundant food and water. I know the seasons, the summer in high pasture and the winter in the lower fields. I provide shelter in times of storms. I will die for them. I call each by name; only a few follow.

The others will prefer the seeming safety of the pen guarded by the dog. However, life in the pen is not safe. The sheep get restless and need to be entertained between meals. The strong sheep are predatory. The fat get fatter; the weak, weaker; death comes, and no one cares. To the caregivers, death is considered a loss of income, an inconvenience. No one loves sheep.

But when following Me, the sheep are fully engaged with the journey; the excitement is in the following. I love having them along.

It is good to spend time exploring the heights with the Shepherd. That imaginary journey led me to think of Psalm 23. I found a prayer I had written based on this Psalm.

Psalm 23

The Lord, my Shepherd, You are worthy to be the only Treasure I ever need. You are so close yet so mysterious.

The glorious One walks before me into the high country, ahead and alert, keeping me safe and secure. It is so great, Lord, that I'm not afraid. Strong and mighty, You lead me into the mountains along steep cliffs, into hidden valleys, and to quiet waters. There is no way I would go alone to these places. I'd be lost and afraid. The vistas and the things that are here are wonderful. Yet being with You is a far greater joy.

I see:
Tiny flowers that grow here
The ancient tree windblown and twisted
The clouds dancing over the ridge
The white mountain goats climbing the rocks

My heart is filled with the swell of melody and words—rhythms and harmonies. I hear Your voice, Your whistle, Your joy.

I'm a child following behind, skipping and running, joyfully singing and chattering with You. Look, the yellow buttercups, the silver doves, the colors of green, blue, and brown.

You make it possible to wonder, to imagine, to rest, to feed upon the sweet grass.

You call,

Come, we must descend. The night is coming. I'll guard you in the sheepfold. Tomorrow we'll leave again, up and beyond the ordinary.

Chapter Twenty

Love—To Give
God's Overflowing, Creative Passion

God so loved the world that He gave His only
begotten Son.
—John 3:16

January 2011—Today is foggy and cold. The dog sleeps by
the fire; the washer and dryer hum away. This chapter is about the
Lord's generous, wonderful love, an overflowing of His very being.
To know Him is the essence of knowing love.

All morning I've had a mind picture of a mighty river cascading
over a precipice: thunderous water pouring over the rocks, boiling
up in eddies, rushing down the riverbed. In the vision I'm standing
below and to one side of the waterfall. The immense power and
volume of this river is seriously scary to me. I tell myself, *Be careful!
Don't get too close to the edge.* Mist fills the air and covers me in its
refreshing spray.

This mind picture illustrates the tremendous power, the
never-ending flow, the life-giving water of God's love. The gentle
mist is His refreshing, covering, and ever-present love that is
comforting and a delight. Experiencing even a little of His mighty
love causes me to hunger "to know the width and length and depth
and height—to know the love of Christ which passes knowledge;
and be filled with all the fullness of God" (Ephesians 3:14-19).

I know, of course, that the genesis of all earthly love is God's great overflowing, unending, and selfless love. Giving and receiving affection and affirmation is a natural, God-given gift. Beyond this inherent love is the extraordinary gift of divine love. This kind of love is not natural; it is much greater, making it possible to love the unlovable, the afflicted, the enemy, and those who are despicable but nonetheless loved by God. Unfortunately, I exhibit even on the best of my days only a small portion of God's kind of love—a love that is pure, intense, deep, and passionate.

———

Lord, You are the One who taught me to love openly, fully, and with great joy. Even after years of Spirit-lessons, it is so difficult for me to love others as You have loved me.

About twenty years ago the little phrase *love—to give* seemed to drop into my mind without my initiation; it was probably one of those God-thoughts, thoughts that open vistas of realization and continuous revelation. I had no comprehension of what these words meant, but I was to find out. My instruction began with my neighbor knocking on the door. "Hey, could I borrow two cups of flour? I'll pay you back after the first of the month when we get paid."

"Sure," I said inviting her in for a cup of coffee.

Well, this little scenario repeated itself at the end of every month for years. I needed to learn to give without expecting anything in return and without complaint or resentment. You would think I could do that. Nope. Outwardly I was gracious and giving, but my thoughts went like this:

Oh, no—here she comes again. I wonder what she wants this time. Month after month, year after year she runs out of stuff at the end of each month. Someone needs to teach her how to manage her money and grocery shopping. Lord, how long is she going to borrow groceries from me?

Until you can give her what she asks for without resentment.

The food—is it yours or Mine? If it is Mine, then you will give it to her without resentment.

But Lord, we run out of things too. Groceries don't grow on trees, especially out here. Keeping a good supply of things is important.

Yes, that is true, but the food—is it yours or Mine?

The issue was not the neighbor's constant borrowing, but my continuous clutching on to the Lord's provision. In reality I didn't want to share anything with her.

Just when I thought I had victory over my resentment, she would come along and ask for something else, an item very precious to me. You name it, she borrowed it: twelve cups of flour, two cups of sugar, a cup of oil, a loaf of bread, five pounds of potatoes, laundry soap, and toilet paper. Of course, the Lord knew right where to put pressure on my clutching fingers.

Let go! Give it to her!

Finally I got it! My neighbor was not irresponsible. I was the one who was unloving and stingy. Oh, dear, Lord, change my heart so I can be genuinely generous.

The lessons were not over. I soon realized I liked to give to some people and not to others. It was natural and fun to share with my family and friends, with people I liked. However, I found my graciousness extended only to those who could give me something in return.

God was not pleased.

Who is in control of your life—you or Me? If I want you to love and spend time with someone you don't like, too bad. Learn to love anyone who comes along. If someone needs shelter, give him or her a sanctuary. It is the afflicted and beaten down who need My love. Are you going to withhold My love from them?

But Lord, what about me?

I'll meet your needs but rarely through the people you give to; many times they have nothing to give. Love—to give! I love you all the time.

Quit being miserly.

It took a long time, but gradually my attitude changed. I really did become more generous. People in great need came to live with us and found sanctuary, love, and a place to heal. I deeply loved them. Then the lesson seemed to be to let them go. Each time I grieved over their leaving; I felt abandoned.

Gently the Lord said:

My dear little friend, I don't want you to be in love with love itself. My love always involves relinquishment. I release the beloved to love others. Love that holds on to the beloved, demanding love in return, kills love. Let go!

My love flows into you. I must be enough. Love . . . to give, is My way. When I died on the cross, My love flowed from My broken body, My bleeding wounds. I loved the Father, and He chose the cross for Me; My obedience released life. I suffered for the beloved. I forgave and released the beloved so they could love others as I have loved. My love is inside of you so you can bless, give, break, and pour out; love—to give.

I'm still learning *love—to give*, a life of giving love, a love that always overflows, that blesses, that welcomes, that creates, that saves. Being a conduit of this love lets me experience the Lord's intense, intimate love and compassion. I've found His love is gentle and comforting, filled with mercy yet invasive and truthful. Seeing through excuse and pretense, He wounds and then heals. His truth brings healing and forgiveness.

Intimacy with God eventually leads to His deep passion, His embrace, His invading closeness of Spirit. "He is not a tame lion, you know!" exclaims Lucy in the *Chronicles of Narnia* by C. S. Lewis. Aslan, a mighty lion, a Christ figure, is fierce as well as tender.

Once in a while Jesus comes into my spirit in a powerful, invasive way. On these occasions I'm catapulted into a domain of holiness, authority, and kindness so all-encompassing it destroys all my fear. A river of revelation, an unveiling of His *knowing* flows into my mind. In this place my unworthiness and uncleanness are stark reality, yet His mercy covers my sin. Weeping, I know His goodness and eternal love. He laughs and celebrates and welcomes me.

Rich and lavish
Generous and joyful

Comforting and honest
Encouraging and strengthening
Precious and intimate

His love—a treasure
He is Love Himself!

Oh, it is good to be welcomed and loved.

Chapter Twenty-One

Father Love

Love That Embraces and Welcomes the Lost

> When he was still a great way off, his father saw him
> and had compassion, and ran and fell on his neck
> and kissed him.
>
> —Luke 15:20

February 2011—The daffodils are showing color, the robins are back, hopping about, tugging at worms stuck in the frozen ground, and the first spring lambs, brilliant white and frisky, spot the green fields. It is clear and very cold—snow is on the way.

Today Cricket and I went for a hike into Brunswick Canyon. As we headed up the trail, past the waterfall at the sandstone cliffs, I heard a bark from what I thought was a small dog. *That's strange.* I thought. *What's a dog doing up there?* Suddenly a coyote, not a dog, came tearing out of the underbrush right in front of us. Cricket took off after him at lightning speed. *Oh no! I hope he comes back.* Anxiously waiting, totally frustrated with his running off, I finally heard a crashing in the underbrush. Sure enough, Cricket appeared, all wild-eyed and soaking wet. What a relief! Delighted to have him back, I scratched him behind the ears and rubbed his under-chin and gave him a treat. We then continued up the hill, ready for a new, adventurous encounter.

Truthfully, I find it hard to let Cricket off-leash because I'm afraid I might lose him, yet he so loves the freedom to dawdle over smells and run after hidden prey. I'm pretty confident he'll return to me eventually, but I don't like the anxious waiting.

Strangely, this little episode paralleled my reading for the morning in Luke chapter fifteen. Jesus, illustrating how God looks for and welcomes home the lost, tells the parable of the prodigal son, a son who left his father and wasted his inheritance in the far-country. Eventually the son returns, no longer lost, no longer dead.

Often the focus in this familiar parable is on the foolish son, the Prodigal Son. However, I think the central figure of this story is the father whose extravagant, lavish, and profuse love perfectly describes Father God.

The Story

The story begins with the younger of two brothers asking for his inheritance so he can leave home and go his own way. The father doesn't give advice, argue, or threaten him. Instead he releases him, all the while knowing trouble will be this son's future; experience will be his teacher.

Ah, love possesses only what it releases.

What a difficult, sad day for any father or mother. Many of us know the agony of those days of separation and anxious waiting.

Finally, after many months, the father sees this son, broken and hungry, coming down the road to home. Not waiting for the knock at the door, the father runs to the son, wild with joy, hugging, kissing, and receiving his lost son into his arms. He covers his naked, starving son with a coat, puts the family signet ring on his finger, and protects his dirty feet with sandals. Home at last, forgiven and welcomed, this lost foolish son is restored. What joy!

The father issues an invitation to all his neighbors and his whole household, "Come, feast with us; my son who was lost is home; he was dead, but now lives."

There was great celebration; the feasting and dancing went far into the night. However, not everyone came to the party. The elder son, returning from the fields, stood aloof, critical, jealous—hating the festivity, resenting his father's joy. The father didn't leave him stewing in bitterness but sought him out. With great graciousness he says, "You have been with me all along, and everything I have is yours. Come; celebrate the return of your brother who was lost, who was dead, but now lives."

Isolated in his self-righteous anger, this dutiful son is now in the far-country, outside the house, alone in his bitterness. The father longs for this son to give up his complaint and join in the family celebration. Will he come back? We are not told, but surely this father is a man of sorrows, acquainted with grief. What an exquisite picture of father-love, the Great Father's love.

———

Jesus, You tenderly spoke about Your Father whose image had become sorely distorted throughout history. You were the living picture of Father God; the picture of a wondrous God, the *Abba* God, Daddy God. Loving Him every moment of every day, Your words and actions were actually those of Your invisible Father. Knowing what pleased Him, what brought Him great joy; You enjoyed Him and listened to His counsel.

Unlike us, Jesus, You never wasted Your Father's provision, nor were You ever proud and judgmental. Your heart was always Father-tuned.

Oh, how You must grieve over us, the self-indulgent foolish ones, the bitter, resentful ones. O Lord, help! Turn us back into the Father's waiting arms. I wonder if we have learned anything in the far-country.

The glorious coat hangs on a peg; the signet ring sits abandoned; the protective sandals are at the doorstep.

The Father waits, watching the empty road.

This morning, as I thought about this parable I felt exposed; my imperfect, fickle love, uncovered.

Father God, I'm so sorry for not listening to Your counsel, grabbing hold of my possessions, running away from You. I'm quite like my silly dog running after coyote, deer, or raccoon, finding a thrill in the chase, the independence. Learning from experience has often brought suffering: wounding, loneliness, poverty of spirit, sickness, temptation, and even the touch of death. The change of heart comes at a high price.

Running back to You, I am brought to bitter tears by Your welcome. I'm a child, broken and humble, loved and treasured by my heavenly Father. Your love is not reserved and appropriate. It is spontaneously exuberant—a welcome filled with kisses and hugs, celebration and provision.

Oh, how good You are!

"The Lord is long-suffering and kind. He rejoices in the truth. While he waits in love, He bears all things, believes all things, hopes all things, and endures all things. Love never fails" (from 1 Corinthians 13:4-8).

Part V

Responsive Obedience

As the Lord became entwined in my life, obedience was my natural response to His desires. As my love deepened for Him, I no longer resented His discipline; rather, I found I wanted to do all He asked of me.

The stories tell of my passage along this trail; I gradually began loving to please the Lord. He taught me to love, to give to those He chose, to be compassionate toward afflicted people, to be honest even if it cost relationship, to persevere in prayer.

Chapter Twenty-Two

Obedience
Run to Do His Will

God, teach me lessons for living so I can stay the course.
Give me insight so I can do what you tell me—my
whole life one long, obedient response.
—Psalm 119:33-34, *The Message*

The Oregon beach is a favorite place of mine. I love the ocean roar, the smell of salty air, the ebb and flow at water's edge, the changing interplay between reflected sky on wet sand, a light and color display. The entire scene is one of change, a kaleidoscope of shapes and colors. Everything is momentary: the flight of birds, the bright color of kites, the dance of the kite surfers, the fleeting sight of crabs and clams burrowing into the sand. Incoming tidal water covers barnacles and starfish, sand and driftwood, and then the ebb of tide uncovers beautiful gardens in tide pools.

I hear the symphony of gull screams piercing through the roar of mighty water and listen with delight to the crackle and pop of round stones rolling up and down the beach to the rhythm of the incoming and outflowing waves. I see the dance of shore birds, sandpipers darting along sea edge. I feel the contrast of warm sand, icy water, and toe-warming tide pools. My feet dig into dry, soft sand as I walk toward the rock-hard surface at water's edge. I enjoy sculpted sand patterns created by wind, displayed in sunlight and shadow.

On any given day fog can cover the land as a dampening cloak can hide walkers and creatures in quiet, lonely spaces. Then suddenly the sun burns holes through the fog blanket, shooting blue, pink, and gold through the mist.

I always sense the Lord's closeness in this wondrous place. I walk along on hard sand in silence with songs of adoration rising and falling in my quiet heart. I'm so glad I can hear and obey His instruction. In fact, it was here years ago I experienced one of the most profound and needed corrections of my life.

Spring Church Retreat, 1994—Escaping for a short time away from a group activity, I sat down in a wind-protected, hidden place among the beach grass. Preparing for this retreat had been a very busy and stressful time. I wanted to quiet my spirit, release the stress of the day, and get ready for ministry.

———

Warmed by the sun and fully enjoying this time alone, I heard the invasive whisper of the Lord,

Why do you resist My calling on your life? I called you before you were born to love Me, to glorify My name, to be a mouthpiece to My people. I created you to be a leader, yet you resist this call. You resent taking responsibility and making decisions, complaining about being alone and carrying the burden of leadership. Instead of enjoying your authority, you resent your placement, wanting someone else to take responsibility and lead. You've done what I've asked of you, but the tasks are difficult because of your resentment.

As I thought about these words, I knew they were true. My mind was flooded with memories of times when I was angry with the Lord for putting me into situations that required my leadership. I would do what He said but resent His intrusion into my life with His plans. But I knew the Lord would root out my presumptuous attitude and my whining complaint. I was in for many, many years of experiences that freed me from my anger.

At this point I got up and went for a walk on the beach, trying to process His true words. It was a beautiful and clear but windy. Heading right into the chilly wind, I confessed my anger to the Lord. I realized I obeyed the Lord but often muttered in my soul about how hard it was to lead other people and make decisions.

As I walked down the beach into the wind, the Lord continued:

When there is no acceptance of your calling—that of a leader—then even when the way is clear, the calling and purpose in place, you are hindered in every way, just as you are now, walking against the wind; there is no ease. Turn around! Walk the other way!

I turned around, retracing my steps. This time the wind was behind me, pushing me along. Not hindered, I moved with ease.

If you live without resentment, life will be like walking down the beach with a tailwind. Everything will be easier. I desire to take you to places you cannot imagine, giving you things to do way beyond your natural ability. Each new assignment will be very difficult unless you relinquish this resentment. If you repent, your life will be empowered by the wind of the Spirit. Leadership is always a lonely walk, but you won't be alone. I will be with you. Be content. Be joyful.

A feeling of quietness and peace came into my heart as I confessed my disobedience and came to grips with the deep root of resentment.

O Lord, help me embrace Your placement of me; may I run to do Your will.

You are now ready to enter into an ever-deepening, inner quietness. This is not silence. This is not detachment.
Wait for wisdom. Be still and know I am God!

This is intense listening.
This is intense discernment.
This is intense knowing.
This is intense learning.
This is intense concentration.

Spring Women's Retreat, 2008—Quite unexpectedly I remembered the day on the beach when the Lord spoke to me about a deep root of resentment that I had. The music was quiet and reverent. I was silent, still, and listening.

Looking back over the past, I saw the gradual process of healing that released me from that anger. I understood I resented the Lord's preeminence, His right to interrupt my time and agenda. I was healed as I relinquished my plans and possessions and then embraced God's intrusions as great opportunities to influence others. I then enjoyed my placement and calling.

In the quiet atmosphere of worship I heard the Joyful Voice once again:

Run! Run at water's edge! Dance with the birds. Splash in the pools; enjoy the wind; listen to the roar of the waves; hear the crackle of the tumbling rocks; see the colors; feel the wind hurrying you along. This is a wonderful, exuberant place to live.

My dear little friend, I am with you always!

Lord, Your goodness overwhelms me. I bow, weeping and remembering all the years of receiving wisdom from Your hand. I'm glad You never give up on me. It has taken years to embrace with contentment the place You have called me to serve. Thank You so much.

"The law of the Lord is perfect, converting the soul; The testimony of the Lord is sure, making wise the simple" (Psalm 19:7).

Chapter Twenty-Three

Kindness
Kiss the Wound

Be kind to one another, tenderhearted, forgiving one
another, even as God in Christ forgave you.
—Ephesians 4:32

April 2011—Each day I wait for the rain to stop so I can
ready the garden for planting, but *nosiree!* It has rained every
day for weeks, and it's cold. I've been able to walk the dog but
only between downpours and hail showers. I see signs of spring
everywhere: trillium, yellow Johnny-jump-ups, purple and white
violets, and unfurling fern fiddleheads. Even the potato eyes in
my cool, dark pantry know it's planting time. Soon, very soon, the
weather will turn warm—time to get the trusty tiller out and get
to work.

Lord, this morning I'm particularly thankful that almost
every day You show me hidden areas in my life that need to
change. By giving me a clear, profound thought that changes
my perspective, I then see from Your viewpoint and hear and
respond to Your Word.

———

"Kiss the Wound" is one of those serendipitous events in which I received a comeuppance from the Lord.

Kiss the Wound

Yesterday morning, while I was in town running errands, I went to a print shop to make several copies of my manuscript. It was a very busy place; people were coming and going, copying tax returns, making advertising fliers, and printing photographs. As I waited for my order, a little drama unfolded.

A woman and her little four-year-old boy came into the center, and the mother set about making her copies. The active, curious youngster explored, watching the machines as they cranked out copies, going behind the counter to talk with an employee, touching various and sundry switches and buttons, opening paper trays, and lying on the floor, looking under the machines. In the wastepaper basket he found some paper trimmings. Twirling them over his head, he danced about the room.

After several minutes of darting here and there, he pushed the outside door open. His mother saw him, "No!" she yelled. "You get back here right now!" His escape was foiled—for the moment. A few minutes later, when his mother was distracted, he darted out the door. Once outside, he immediately wanted back inside. As he came back in, his hand got caught between the swinging doors. He was trapped. His piercing scream got his mother's attention. Dropping what she was doing, she charged across the room, freed his hand, dragging him over to her workstation. Soundly scolding him for his disobedience, showing no pity for his wound, she plunked him down and returned to her work. Tears were trickling down his chubby cheeks, and he was holding his reddened, pinched fingers in his mouth. His crying died to a whimper. After several minutes of hiccups and sniveling, looking up from his misery, he noticed me watching him. Coming over, he held up his little hand, showing me his wound. I leaned over and gently kissed his little fingers. Even though still sniffling, he gave me a little grin and then ran back to his mother.

Believe it or not, this little encounter changed my life. Immediately after the child left, I had an absolutely clear and simple thought: *You kissed the wound of this little boy, showing kindness to him even though he had been disobedient to his mother. Why don't you show the same kindness and mercy to adults who make foolish, ill-advised decisions?*

Startled by this revealing question, I was cut to the heart. Truly, showing mercy is not one of my natural strengths. When confronted with someone who should know better, or who never learns, or who makes decisions that hurt others, I immediately want to scold, correct, and remind just like a harried mother. All too often I say what I'm thinking and leave the person wounded and discouraged. I'm appalled by this hardness of heart.

I'm thankful the Holy Spirit convicts me of my impatience and judgmental attitude. He reminds me that God is very patient with me when I fail or disobey or make bad choices. Now, when I see someone stumble or get hurt as a direct result of foolishness, I remember the little smashed fingers and my sympathetic kiss of comfort. I hear the Spirit remind me once again, *Kiss the wound.* This stops me in my tracks. I then have the grace to gently touch the person with a little mercy and kindness.

Heaven knows there have been times in my own life when I have made bad choices, cried bitter tears, and desperately needed a compassionate hug. Friends have come alongside, giving me strength, commiserating with my wounds, and being there to help me forgive myself, start over, and guide me through the entangled mess of my own making. I'm so glad for mercy, especially when I deserve a good scolding. I am forever in debt to my kind friends.

Sometimes a little instruction is in order. However, I'm learning when someone is smarting from "smashed fingers," it is not particularly a good time for lectures. Later, much later, an opportunity might present itself for a little dose of truth. Then it is often possible to help another person learn a new way of doing things.

This morning, as I wrote about this little drama, I thought, *Wouldn't it have been wonderful if the mother in this little drama had included her son in her work?* I can just see her lifting him up so he could see what she was doing. She could have let him load the paper, push the buttons, and collect the copies from the tray. Most children are anxious to learn and help. Focused on her task, she didn't include him. Hmmm—sounds familiar.

———

Lord, thank You for this wonderful lesson, so simple and yet so hard to apply. Help me see with Your eyes and love with Your heart, enjoying people and their explorations. Let me be kind to them, showing mercy at their blunders, and encouraging them to enthusiastically explore their worlds. Soften my heart, Lord, so I might show others Your kindness and give them space to wrestle with hard decisions and then make their own choices.

Chapter Twenty-Four

Compassion
To Suffer With

*Finally, all of you be of one mind, having compassion
for one another; love as brothers, be tenderhearted,
be humble; not returning evil for evil or reviling for
reviling, but on the contrary blessing,
knowing that you were called to this,
that you may inherit a blessing.*
—1 Peter 3:8-9

It had been a long season of despair—suddenly this morning, a miracle! Bob softly whistles an old jazz tune as he works on an exquisite, peaceful, light-filled painting. Oh, goodness—I haven't heard Bob whistling for ages. His dark season of depression might be over, but I'm not sure at this point. It's been years since he's smiled or laughed. Depression grips him; the spirit of death robs him of delight, success, and hope. He works everyday torn in indecision—silent, withdrawn, and miserable. Hearing Bob's melodious whistle brings me great joy; maybe the cycle of despair is starting to break.

Even though Bob seems to be getting better, Lord, I continue to struggle; hope lies dormant in my heart. I wrestle with isolation and oppression. This has been a wicked season of disappointment and fear for me. It's as if I've been pulled through a knothole. Everything I love, everyone I love has been stripped from me.

Lord, I know it's Your doing, but I'm not happy; I've fought, argued, and cried bitter tears.

Now I feel empty except for a huge pool of sorrow. The loss is enormous: loss of friends, church, a platform of influence, my good reputation, income, ministry, access into people's lives, and my trust of others. I've been killed off by whispered gossip, betrayal by close friends, manipulation and malicious disregard. I know I am to extend mercy and forgiveness. At the same time there are things worth standing for—truth and righteousness.

———

This was the season of despair that occurred several years ago. Yet even here there was a delightful surprise. The Lord in His unique way brought a spot of sunshine, a gift, a golden retriever puppy. This was the Lord's way of reminding us that in seasons of sorrow there are things of joy, reminders of other times of happiness.

The Story of Triple Gold

This puppy is a light yellow fluff-ball filled with joyful energy, mischief, and tail-wagging affection. What fun! I feel happy and thankful while I am with him. This dog is pure joy and exuberance. Running at full speed, he circles the orchard and house. I hear him coming and see a flash of white tail as he bursts past. Always leading the way, the point-man, he and I hike in the watershed canyons. Absolutely loving water, he'll jump into the creek in any kind of weather, retrieving a stick or trying to find the beaver that slaps its tail and disappears. He flushes out quail but never catches any; the tiny chicks scatter before him like dust balls. In winter he snowplows, running with his nose down in the snow—so many memories, such delight, my only happiness during this season.

However, as I write this several years after his death, I know he was a gift for just a season. "The Lord gives and the Lord takes away." Like all temporal things, Triple would soon be no more. During his life I learned to love and enjoy him. Then I learned compassion by suffering alongside him during his sickness and death.

Compassion, suffering with another, is the lesson I learned in the coming weeks.

March 28, 2001—While petting Triple, my fingers find lymph nodes the size of small lemons in his neck. Immediately I'm sick at heart, fearing he has lymphoma. The veterinarian confirms my fear, giving us dreadful news. "He has only days to live. He might just have a massive infection instead of cancer, but I don't think so."

We take him home and wait. He is very sick.

O God, I can hardly stand this. Sorrow and fear grip my heart. My yellow dog that whirls and dances may soon lie still. The pain of losing my faithful friend rips me open. Tears pour down my face, soaking my shirt. O God, no! Please make him well again.

Sorrow is one octave on the keyboard. I desire to play all the keys so that My compassion can be expressed through you. It is only then that love can flow to others who suffer.

April 6, 2001—My broken heart is silent, weighted down, heavy with grief. I feel the warm, furry, soft head of Triple and weep, knowing his life will diminish. A raw hope hides behind my more practical side that understands he will die. My prayer is that somehow what has been proclaimed (his imminent death) will not happen so he can run and dance, swim and live.

His nose nuzzles my fingers. I gently caress him as I suffer. I carry a heavy heart. My prayers are for healing. My hope is for health. I am undone and unable to love enough. Each day is given to show him love, spending time giving and helping and praying. His loyalty, sweet devotion, and joy at my presence break my heart, yet compassion means to walk beside, carry the weight, to suffer with him until the end.

Days go by; waiting—watching—dreading—hoping, the essence of suffering—the work of compassion. Nothing moves through me but pure sorrow.

April 22, 2001—Thanks Lord—Triple is still alive and seems better. He was able to go down to the bamboo farm—to swim—to fetch—to run. He seems to be gaining strength; his fever is down, and he is friskier. My prayer—that I would have time before his death to love him—has been answered. He is very quiet, devoted and affectionate, joyful and welcoming.

This is so hard for me to just be there for him all the while knowing I'm going to lose him. I must face the fear of death, the anger of losing this gift the Lord so graciously gave me. He has become such a symbol of vim and vigor, joy and exuberance, health and happiness during this otherwise dark season. The joyful moments will be gone. Oh, Lord, please help me.

Last night as I read *The Life of the Beloved* by Henri Nouwen, Triple came and curled up on my feet just to be with me—to make contact, to rest in a warm, safe place, to be still. This illustrates beautifully how we can be with the Lord; it also illustrates how we are to be with one another.

My dog is dying; my tears drip on his head. I ruffle his golden fur and rub his soft, white muzzle. Deep, way deep inside, I grieve. I remember him healthy, agile, and fast, a yellow flash of boundless energy and pure joy. In my memory he still dances through puddles, whirls in snow, shakes ice crystals from his fur, and naps in a puddle after a long hike.

April 26, 2001—Lord, thanks for my golden dog. He went completely blind, hemorrhaging inside his eyes. He quietly died as we watched the veterinarian put him to sleep. I'll write more when the tears don't come so easily.

Thanks for all You do for me, so much and so constantly. During this time I naturally loved Triple, a care arising out of his dependence and love for me.

He rests in a high place in the woods. He had a noble death, so sweet in his last days. On his last night with me we sat for a long time on the porch. He laid his head on my lap, resting, enjoying my touch, and comforting me in my sorrow. I watched the evening light fade and thought of the night walk, the intensely quiet place filled with nature's songs and millions of stars.

April 28, 2001—Gentle, rainy morning: sorrow sits in my heart like a rising flood, overflowing in tears. The grief is pure—no anger—no regret—no mixed feelings. A beautiful love lies in the grave, no longer with me. Memories flood in, bringing joy, delight, softness in my heart. There is silence in the deep place. All is well; loss is part of love. There is no way to deeply love without pain.

Lord, I know You have been trying to give me a sense of permanence, beyond the loss. My focus is always on the wondrous delight of someone or something—treasuring what comes into my life from Your hand. When an end comes and the change occurs, I grieve the loss. I must see beyond the gift.

Gift-giver, You are always present and always giving perfect gifts for our enjoyment. Lord, help me remember You are the Gift, the One we love, the One who lives beyond earth's time. Change comes; in a moment the precious is no longer. The last days of Triple were wondrously tender, a great love affair. He is gone, but You are present to comfort, to compassionately love me. I walk alone once again. Tears come easily, but I have learned to love in a deeper way, to be compassionate with the suffering ones.

"Your gentleness has made me great" (Psalm 18:35).

Chapter Twenty-Five

Be Honest

Compassion One Side of Love—
Truth the Other

Only in returning to me and waiting for me will you
be saved; in quietness and confidence is your strength.
Do not say, "We will get our help from Egypt."
Yet the Lord still waits for you to come to Him, so he
can show you his love.
He will conquer you to bless you, just as He said.
—Isaiah 30:15-18, *TLB*

June 2011—I know my assignment for life is first to love the
Lord with my whole heart and then to love people. Sounds so
simple, yet it is impossible without the empowerment of the Holy
Spirit. Ah, once again I must remember just how little I know and
how dependent and needy I am. Without constant conversation
with the Lord and the counsel of Your Word and Spirit, I have
nothing life-changing to say and no power to do anything.

Lord, I sincerely hope when people are with me they
experience Your presence and not just my meager attempt at being
loving. Lord, Help!

Every human is incomplete and in need of My love. However, people often like to believe they can handle life without My help. It is the disheartened, wounded, grieving, those who are at wit's end and in desperate need who most often know they need someone to save them. I then have access into their hearts, and real change takes place. It is into these situations I send you and My other friends to personally love these wounded and needy people.

Being with and sharing life with brokenhearted, desperate people is a great privilege, yet I've found it very difficult. I've hit potholes of betrayal, fallen off the Lord's path into unwise decisions, gotten ensnared in dependent relationships, hated and loved at the same time, and totally become so wounded at losing some people to the enemy that I've withdrawn from them and quit trying to be there for them. Yet it is here that I've seen the Lord's power invade the despairing ones and bring them strength, truth, and healing.

Lord, why do I find it hard to love these very ones assigned to me?

You don't like to be uncomfortable. Loving those who are needy and who draw from you always involves relinquishment and sacrifice. You want to be liked and appreciated and have answers that bring immediate relief so you can return to your comfortable life.

God, that's so true! Change my heart. Let me give honor and credence to their suffering.

As You know, Lord, I'm in the middle of a very difficult situation. The more I try to help my friends, the worse it gets. What can I do?

No one naturally has My kind of love; it comes from My Father. Only by My Spirit will you be able to truly love these discouraged and angry people. My love can penetrate into the very heart of the matter, to the real need, the vital human need to be loved unconditionally.

I realize I must be compassionate, but there comes a time when truth must be spoken. I find it easier to be friendly and loving, avoiding any confrontation. It is far more difficult for me to listen to the Spirit, discern the real problem, and then share the Lord's deep and penetrating insight. His truth carries with it the power to bring change, healing the heart at a deep level. I know circumstances are never the real issue; the heart-set determines whether help is received from the Lord or from substitutes.

"The Lord still waits for you to come to Him, so he can show his love. He will conquer you to bless you, just as He said" (Isaiah 30:15-18, *TLB*).

It is difficult for me to be the Lord's representative, His real presence, an instrument of His love. The ones in need of healing push me away with their suppressed anger, boiling hatred, and paralyzing discouragement. When their demand for answers, quick fixes, and anything that relieves the pain is not forthcoming, they turn and attack. Also, I'm never sure what I know and see is correct.

Today, as I thought about this current situation, I found the answer to this dilemma in *My Utmost for His Highest* by Oswald Chambers: "The battle is won or lost in the secret places of the will before God, never in the external world. The Spirit of God apprehends me and I am obliged to get alone with God and fight the battle out before Him. Until this is done, I lose every time."[9]

It looks like I need to get serious about seeking the Lord instead of fretting and doubting His ability to straighten things out. He is the only Healer who can penetrate the thick, protective walls and get to the bottom of things. Behavior is only a symptom of what is askew underneath. As I pray, His grace will enable eyes to open, hearts to soften. That grace without limit, eternal, full of power, will continue expanding and multiplying. I often miss the Lord's magnificent answers to prayer because I look only for a specific solution instead of ongoing grace—the ever-expanding answer.

---

[9]   Oswald Chambers, *My Utmost For His Highest* (New York: Dodd, Mead, 1963), 184.

Unfortunately, it is easy for me to act as if I'm the savior. I've found that my good intentions are usually not the Lord's. Too often my motivation is to fix the person, get the job done, and then return to my life. I realize healing is never about getting things done; instead, it's developing a caring and truthful relationship with someone, bringing him or her into a relationship with Jesus. Then it is possible to rejoice and praise the Lord as He heals and delivers.

It is so easy for me to feel superior. When I start thinking, *If you both would just . . .* , then I know I'm being prideful. Who am I to tell someone else what to do or to think? I know the Lord always goes to the core of the difficulty even if things stay messy for a long time. In fact, love is sometimes not enough; choice remains with others! The Lord never takes that freedom of choice away. I want to snatch it away and fix the problem.

Lord, what should I do when Your truth is disregarded?

The response to My directive is not your responsibility. Speak the truth; don't compromise My word.

Lord, I see suffering and destruction ahead for them. I'm deeply grieved.

You must stop trying to be helpful; just be honest. Leave the results to Me. Bring the truth not to fix, not to be helpful, but to bring a standard, a warning. Then step away—wait—pray.

It is My job to bring salvation.

Remember you do not have the power or wisdom to solve problems. You hate this place of helplessness; embrace your own limitations. Stop trying to make things right. It is your job to stay in My presence, waiting, watching, and praying. As you stand back and wait, you will eventually see miracles as My truth takes root and grows.

Do not lose heart, My little friend.

Chapter Twenty-Six

Resurrection Life
Continue in Prayer

Then the same day at evening, being the first day
of the week when the doors were shut where the
disciples were assembled for fear of the Jews, Jesus
came and stood in the midst, and said to them,
"Peace be with you."

—John 20:19

July 2011—When close, spiritual relationships change from intimate to casual I become sad, frustrated, and discouraged. I want to have continual, close fellowship with others, yet this never happens.

Over the years there have been wondrous, precious gatherings of dear friends. The relationships with them grew from casual to intimate and delightful friendships. Often the Lord was the center of conversation. It was glorious—the sharing of what He was doing and how His Word was applicable to our situations. There was a free exchange of ideas, hopes and prayers, insights and struggles.

This kind of friendship is the best—so rare and so precious. Here the Lord's love penetrates the walls of separation, making it possible to share our lives with others. It is in this atmosphere that friends become grafted into our hearts by the Spirit. Fickle, human love transforms into the unconditional love that comes from God. This kind of friendship is creative, restorative, and extraordinary.

I've noticed it is only as I open my own spirit to the Lord's incredible presence that I experience this kind of love. When I expect to hear from Him, quiet my inner self, it is then His Spirit flows into my spirit—new, creative thoughts materialize, worshipful songs rise from deep in my heart, and truth becomes apparent. This powerful influx of Spirit results in a concentration of quietness; a quickening of my spirit-ear occurs in a quest for mystery. As a result I experience those things not evident in the natural but quite ordinary in the spiritual world.

In this stillness of heart there comes a great awareness of others, a wondrous longing for my friends to receive the Lord's quieting peace, overflowing joy, and unconditional love. Sometimes His love flows across my spirit into others; His love jumps the gap, so to speak, enabling them to experience the Spirit as He flows from my spirit. His life bathes us in glorious presence.

In this intimate fellowship we learn so much. There is a wellspring of revelation, a river of insight and wisdom. Unadulterated honesty breaks the strong walls of separation. Thanksgiving, praise, worship, high praise, awesome silence takes place; time disappears.

These times give us a touch of what is in the Lord's heart: His burdens, His desires, His purpose, and His joy and love.

Today I finally realized this kind of fellowship with these special friends is over and may not occur again. Access has slowly eroded. Although I wanted to deny the change, I recognize they are now just acquaintances, no longer close friends. When I do see them, the conversation is strained and awkward.

"Hi, how are you?"

"Isn't the weather great?"

"We finally got that car we've been wanting."

"Did you see the news about . . . ?"

"We'll have to get together sometime."

There aren't inquiries or answers. There is chatter without substance. We see each other less and less frequently. In fact there is an avoidance of relationship, a pretending the fellowship never happened or was not real—a figment of imagination, emotional nonsense.

I'm sick at heart, and the grief is intense. It's as if I'm on my knees, wailing, beating on a door that has been slammed shut. I try again and again to gain entrance, but to no avail. What had been wide-open access to the inner place, the dwelling of Spirit, is now closed, the door shut tight. I'm brokenhearted, and I hate the boundary that has been created.

Human love is so fragile, and when there is that unconditional love between people caused by the presence of the Spirit, it is so rare, so extraordinarily beautiful. I want it to last. Am I just in love with the experience?

———

You really do love the atmosphere of My Spirit. You enjoy My love, and when you are with others the joy increases until you cannot contain it. This is life as it should be.

Why doesn't this fellowship last?

When there is fellowship in My Spirit, personal human agendas end. I am the focus, not people. My Word requires a response. When My power transcends human bounds, it usually meets with resistance. A power struggle occurs. Choice belongs to those who are present. The intensity of My presence is difficult for people to bear, thus the resistance, the shutting out, the focus on earthly things.

The truth that has been revealed must be processed, and this takes time. Remember, truth is most often received negatively at first. The heart must wrestle with it before there is obedience. The doors to their spirits close, access disappears.

You have asked to know Me, the power of My resurrection, and the fellowship of My suffering. The resistance and rejection you are now experiencing is part of My suffering.

As you sense the loss of this kind of relationship, pray. The closed door doesn't mean all is lost. Resurrection life goes through closed doors.

It is time for you to be still and know I'm at work.

Ah Lord, being human is so difficult. I want to be with my friends, yet I know You have called me to carry these dear ones in my heart, praying always, giving thanks for their salvation and faithfulness.

Responsive obedience requires me to intercede through thick and thin, but I often want to quit caring. Yet I know Your love is eternal and continues through the struggles. Our inability to walk, continuously responding to Your desires, causes so much sorrow. My faith often fails. I feel like pounding on the door and wailing.

Get up and stop fretting, continue learning My way, love others, and persevere in prayer.

"The steadfast love of the Lord never ceases; His mercies never come to an end. They are new every morning, new every morning. Great is Your faithfulness, O Lord, great is Your faithfulness!" (from Lamentations 3).

Chapter Twenty-Seven

Endurance
Go up Higher

Let us lay aside every weight, and the sin which so
easily ensnares us, and let us run with endurance
the race that is set before us, looking unto Jesus, the
author and finisher of our faith, who for the joy that
was set before Him endured the cross, despising the
shame, and has sat down at the right hand of the
throne of God.
—Hebrews 12:1-2

October 2011—I'm thankful for the race, this extraordinary journey with the Lord. At seventy-one, my earthly life is almost over, old age is ahead, yet I know the adventure has just begun. The race continues through death into eternity.

It seems to me much of the race through life is routine, tedious, open space—yet it is during these simple times that the tests come. Will I be faithful in little things? Honesty, thoroughness, gratitude, and thoughtfulness of others? Discipline and practice of making right choices is the school for endurance.

Have I run the race full out, with vigor, pressing toward the goal? I'm not sure. Many times I've gotten tired and felt like quitting. However, in kingdom racing, quitting is part of the plan. I do know without the Lord's help it would be easy to get waylaid and off track. When I pay attention, the Spirit is able to warn me of danger before I get snared or mortally wounded. I'm able, so to speak, to dash down the trail, up the hill, over the streams, and climb out of dark crevices running through ordinary life endued with grace. Whew!

How the race is run is just as important as the finish. There are no shortcuts in this long race with its switchbacks, ups and downs, and heart-stopping dangers. Sometimes I feel like sprinting to the end, but then I remember the race never ends.

I love this passage of scripture: "Keep on doing what we told you to do to please God, not in a dogged religious plod, but in a living, spirited dance" (I Thessalonians 4:1, *The Message*). O Lord, let it be so!

During most of my adult life I've been a forerunner, one who finds the way through life, traversing an invisible path found only by listening for the Spirit's guidance. I'm still learning to quietly watch, wait, and find my way, directed by the Spirit and empowered by the life of Another, Life from the eternal realm. Gaining some wisdom, I can then counsel those coming along behind me, showing them the Way through their own wildernesses.

Endurance requires natural discipline, strength, and resources, yet these are often not enough. Sometimes I'm worn to a frazzle; I hope the race is over. Then when I'm utterly done in, the Lord gives me His strength—endurance, grit, gumption, and courage—to tackle the problems. Needy and dependent, I never seem to remember His resources are completely sufficient to meet every need I might have. What a miraculous way to live!

How to run this kind of race is learned from our Father and no other way. This is how You, Jesus, endured so much difficulty, living by the life of Your Father. He was the one who blessed and anointed You to run through wilderness and devils, human hatred and betrayal, disease and captivity, wickedness and violence. You ran the race without fear, rebellion, or argument. "Though He was a Son, yet He learned obedience by the things which He suffered" (Hebrews 5:8).

At the end of Your earthly life, the pace intensified through accusation, abandonment, and finally death. In eternity our Father greeted You: "Welcome home My beloved Son! I am well pleased. Jesus, Lord of heaven and earth, the victory is Yours!" (author's paraphrase of Philippians 2:10-11).

Ah, I can hardly wait to see our Father, know His pleasure, and hear, "Welcome! Good race, My little friend." What a great reward that will be! Until then my race continues.

Several years ago I learned the hard way about my own endurance and God's supernatural strength. I remember well that cold March day when I went for an ill-advised hike up into the wilderness near our home.

Go up Higher

March 2011—My goodness, did I ever have an adventure yesterday. It was chilly on this March afternoon (it had snowed during the night). At about one in the afternoon I whistled for the dog, and we began our long hike. We took the usual route up a logging road for a couple of miles. As we gained altitude, the road became snow covered, the puddles iced over. At the place I usually turn back toward home I decided to leave the main road and take the path another quarter mile alongside Williams Creek into Brunswick Canyon to the old beaver dams. Here I crossed over the creek on an ancient log bridge, intending to walk the quarter mile back to the main road on the far side of the creek. Oh, brother, little did I know how difficult this would be.

Because of the steep canyon walls on this far side of the creek, it was not long before I came to a deep ravine with rushing water at its bottom tumbling down the steep incline into the main creek. In order to safely cross without getting wet, I had to climb several hundred feet on a deer trail at the edge of the ravine before the trail crossed the stream. I clung to a vine maple branch, stepped on slippery, ice-covered rocks, and safely made it to the other side.

At this point I should have turned around and gone back the way I had come, but no, I continued on. The deer trail veered northeast, ascending another hundred feet, and then it crossed over another deep ravine. Beautiful icicles hung from rocks and moss. I crossed this ravine and continued until coming to yet another tiny, cascading creek.

Now I'm getting worried.

Lord? Should I continue on or go back?

Go up higher!

So heading northeast (home was southwest), I followed the edge of this ravine that elevated vertically until there was a safe crossing point. The snow was deeper; the way more treacherous.

Again I heard,

Go up higher!

I again followed the edge of this ravine higher and higher and then safely crossed the stream. Continuing northeast, I finally came upon an open, well-used, wide trail that led south under a canopy of ancient trees to a viewpoint, a thousand feet above the valley floor. The short way home was straight down, but it was extremely dangerous because of underbrush and downfalls. The longer but safer way home was a logging road that descended gradually in half-mile switchbacks.

I chose the winding road; it was at least four miles to the main trail where I rested. The dog plopped down and promptly fell asleep. The light was rapidly fading, and it was still another two miles to home. I took my boots off, rubbed my feet, put my boots back on, rested a bit more, and then in the deepening darkness, exhausted, footsore, I limped toward home and arrived just before six.

Well, what did I learn that cold March day? Fortunately, I had done many things correctly. My preparation for the trip had been quite adequate. I had developed physical endurance by hiking several times a week for many years. I was wise enough to wear warm, waterproof clothes and boots and to take water, food, and emergency covering. I was very familiar with the terrain and knew to stay on either deer or elk trails while crossing rough ground. Climbing higher allowed me to cross the ravines safely.

However, I should never have been alone on this trip. It was not my finesse that made the story end well, it was pure grace. Without the Lord's help I probably would have spent a cold, scary night on the mountain. Needless to say, my family would have been greatly distressed.

"Go up higher!" is an imperative of utmost importance. It is in the simplest tasks that I need to go higher, to receive help, to run God's race His way. I have questions: Will I be paying attention to the Lord so I can actually hear Him when He speaks? Will I listen? Will I obey? On this day I heard the Spirit, listened to His counsel, and followed directions—a great feat for me.

Thanks Lord, for the adventure, the good guidance, endurance beyond my strength. Thanks for getting me home in time for supper. And thanks for happy rest.

> I will rejoice in the Lord; I will exult in the God of my salvation! The Lord God is my strength, my personal bravery, and my invincible army; He makes my feet like hinds' feet and will make me to walk (not to stand still in terror, but to walk) and make (spiritual) progress upon my high places (of trouble, suffering, or responsibility)! (Habakkuk 3:18-19 *AMP*)

Part VI

Focus

Our focus determines what and who we become. We become like the one we worship.

If I set my heart to seek the Lord and His kingdom, everything else finds its rightful place.

Preoccupation with all the things of this world can consume all our time, our resources, and our energy. Strangely, even when things seem to be coming our way, in an instant what was so important eventually becomes irrelevant. Only the things of the Holy Spirit are eternal and worth the pursuit.

O Lord, let my focus be upon you, Jesus!

Chapter Twenty-Eight

The Seeking Heart
That I May Know Him

For my determined purpose is that I may know
Him (that I may progressively become more deeply
and intimately acquainted with Him, perceiving and
recognizing and understanding the wonders of His
Person more strongly and more clearly.)
—Philippians 3:10, *AMP*

August 18, 2011—I was standing in the kitchen, looking out the window into the woods behind our house when a slight movement of the leaves caught my eye. Something was on the ground, hidden in the shaded green of thimbleberry, Oregon grape, and ferns. A soft murmur came from the same spot. What is it? I wondered. Getting my 12x Bushnell binoculars, I focused on the shadowed place. My goodness, it was a family of red-shafted flickers. Two adult birds were feeding three chicks big fat grubs from a rotting log. How great to actually observe these furtive birds feeding their young!

These large woodpeckers are spectacular in color: the wings are gray, brown, and black striped with orange-yellow or red wing linings. The underbody has black dots on white with a black bib on the upper chest; the back is white, the head brown and gray with red headbands, the beak long and sharp, perfect for pecking apart rotten wood and snapping up grubs and termites.

Thanks, Lord, for this rare sighting! I'm glad my eye caught the action; my ear heard the quiet sound. I'm thankful for the binoculars so I could focus on the camouflaged birds. Thanks that I'm interested in things like this and that I have the time to observe and enjoy Your critters.

Meditation on John 17

This morning I read Jesus' amazing prayer in John 17. The first three words, "It is time!" particularly drew my attention. I noticed the change point.

Jesus had already said farewell to His followers: "I'm going to the Father, but you'll see me again." He had told them about the gift of the Holy Spirit who would come after His death and resurrection. He joyfully celebrated His last Passover meal and the first Eucharist, a supper of grace and thanksgiving. The new covenant was instituted; the time of instruction and fellowship with His disciples was over; an interlude of great warfare and passion was coming.

Jesus then turned from His disciples and focused on His Father. "It is time!" Jesus prayed. "Glorify Your Son, that Your Son also may glorify You, as You have given Him authority over all flesh, that He should give eternal life to as many as You have given Him. And this is eternal life, that they may know You, the only true God, and Jesus Christ whom You have sent" (John 17:1-3). All the praise, adoration, and honor men could confer on Jesus would be left behind. Earth's glory, limited and nearsighted, would not sustain the Son during the approaching agony of the cross.

Jesus prays, "And now, Father, glorify me with your very own splendor, the very splendor I had in your presence before there was a world" (John 17, *The Message*).

As Jesus carried out the will of the Father, dying on the cross, the Father's mighty strength and love, courage and confidence, peace and authority were available to the Son.

Death filled the empty shell of Jesus' body; heaven and earth waited. It was Sabbath, the time between death and resurrection. And then the intense brilliance and blinding energy of the Father flowed into the total blackness of the tomb. Yes! Now all could see the Father's glory!

The Question: What Do I Want?

As I read this scripture, I remembered when my own focus radically changed from preoccupation with worldly things to a concentration upon the things of God. After much struggle and outright rebellion, I finally surrendered to the Lord. I had been a Christian for years, always striving to be a good person. It never occurred to me I was self-centered and self-focused. Without the Spirit changing my heart I would have shuffled along, fretting about how to be wonderful and how to get my way.

When the foundational and ultimately important shift occurred, my life was no longer about what I wanted, what I thought, what I needed, what I knew, or what I achieved. God became the focus; what He desired became what I wanted. I changed. What I thought important no longer was worth worrying about.

I learned *if I set my heart to seek the Lord and His kingdom, everything else found its rightful place.* Thanksgiving and love naturally overflowed from my life into others.

A. W. Tozer writes,

> While we are looking at God we do not see ourselves. The man who has struggled to purify himself and has had nothing but repeated failures will experience real relief when he stops tinkering with his soul and looks away to the Perfect One. While he looks at Christ, the very things he has so long been trying to do will be getting done within him. It will be God working in him to will and to do . . . The triune God will be our

dwelling place even while our feet walk the low road of simple duty here among men.[10]

Peter Lord writes in his prayer manual,

> If we allow our gaze to be on our request, it will dominate our prayers. We will tell God what we see and what needs to be done. However, if our gaze is upon God, we will ask Him to interpret the situation from His viewpoint (that is, tell us what He sees) and tell us what he wants done.[11]

David writes in Psalm 27, "The Lord is my light and my salvation; whom shall I fear? The Lord is the strength of my life; of whom shall I be afraid?" David later states his one desire:

> One thing I have desired of the Lord, that will I seek; that I may dwell in the house of the Lord all the days of my life, to behold the beauty of the Lord, and to inquire in His temple. For in the time of trouble He shall hide me in His pavilion; in the secret place of His tabernacle He shall hide me; He shall set me high upon a rock. (Psalm 27:1, 4-6)

———

My little friend, what is it you seek?

In the Word, I seek to know Father and Son more deeply and intimately.
In spirit, I seek to hear what is in Your heart.
In life experience, I seek to learn Your way.

---

[10] DeVern Fromke, *Life's Ultimate Privilege,* (Cloverdale, Ind.:), Day 10, p. 5.
[11] Ibid.

In relationships, I seek to love with Your love.

In prayer, I seek the Father's insight and wisdom.

In communion, I seek to remember Your suffering.

In worship, I seek to be thankful and adore Father, Son, and Spirit.

There is a dwelling place, a place of peace in the midst of chaos. The journey and experience of intense quietness opens the way into this dwelling place, a place in God's presence. I'm convinced the disciplines of listening, hearing, responding, knowing, discerning, and focusing on the Lord are in essence *learning the new language of the kingdom*. Experiencing God's presence leads to ever-increasing revelation and multiplied provision, instant wisdom and reassuring peace.

Chapter Twenty-Nine

In His Presence
Joy Unspeakable and Full of Glory

And the Word became flesh and dwelt among us, and
we beheld His glory, the glory as of the only begotten
of the Father, full of grace and truth.

—John 1:14

I'm so thankful for the gift of the Holy Spirit, who reveals the Father and Son to me. I see God's handiwork everywhere. What a gift! I could be blind, or deaf, or hardhearted, or preoccupied, but instead the Holy Spirit has worked in my life in such a way that I can see and hear, I can know and appreciate God's presence. Also, while reading the Scriptures, I receive Spirit-inspired bursts of revelation, thoughts and insights, help and conviction. As if this is not magnificent enough, the Spirit at times crowds close, so to speak, touching me with His gracious gentleness and tender mercy and kindness.

In addition to these quiet, ever-present touches from God, there are rare and extraordinary God-times, astonishing times, so spectacularly unbelievable that words do not describe the phenomenon. The Holy Spirit bursts onto the scene with manifestations of His heavenly glory. I become filled with love for the Lord; I am completely dumbstruck yet bathed in peace and overflowing with joy. "Oh, give thanks to the Lord, for He is good! For His mercy endures forever" (Psalm 118:1).

In church one Sunday morning during a baby dedication, I was suddenly overshadowed by the Holy Spirit; I cannot explain the experience in any other way. As I came forward to join the pastor in prayer for this couple and their eight-day-old daughter, I was very inexplicably filled with the most incredible love for this child. As I held her, the Holy Spirit whispered, *Isn't she wonderful! I love all created life.* God's warmth and power, love and joy splashed over me and onto the parents, the baby, and the congregation. We all responded with weeping and rejoicing, thanksgiving and praise. I was so surprised and completely amazed by this taste of glory.

During these times of the Spirit's manifestation the atmosphere often becomes charged with creativity. My mind fills with song, poetry, and beautiful images. Language seems to be much more fluid and facile, descriptive and insightful. I can write or draw or sing new things. If I meditate on the Word, whole areas of application become apparent. It is wonderful; it is completely God-initiated and way beyond my natural capabilities.

Whenever God is present in this unusual way, I experience His love for me and for others, a love that is deep and passionate, tender and truthful, merciful and good. I'm filled with emotions deeper, richer, truer, and wiser than my own. If I happen to be praying with a person, this love, His passionate love, touches the person, changing his or her disorder to order, despair to hope, and isolation to belonging. I am filled with joy and astonishment, for truly I'm in the presence of Holy God.

In *My Utmost for His Highest,* Oswald Chambers writes,

> No man on earth has this passionate love of the Lord Jesus unless the Holy Spirit has imparted it to him. We may admire Him, we may respect Him, and reverence Him, but we cannot love Him. The only lover of the Lord Jesus is the Holy Ghost and He sheds abroad the very love of God in our hearts.

> Whenever the Holy Spirit sees a chance of glorifying Jesus, he will take your heart, your nerves, your whole

personality, and simply make you blaze and glow with devotion to Jesus Christ.[12]

Unfortunately, much of life is filled with discord and disagreement, sorrow and heartache. It is absolutely wonderful when a tiny bit of God's peace is present; at that time jagged, ripped emotional wounds begin to heal. In their place is *shalom,* the Hebrew word for "completeness, wholeness, peace, health, welfare, safety, soundness, tranquility, prosperity, perfection, fullness, rest, harmony; the absence of agitation or discord."[13] It is as if *Shalom* Himself comes to commune with us, bringing ease and chasing away worry and fear, for He surely is in charge and able to solve all difficulties.

Paul writes to the believers in Colossi and Laodicea,

> I want you woven into a tapestry of love, in touch with everything there is to know of God. Then you will have minds confident and at rest, focused on Christ, God's great mystery. All the richest treasures of wisdom and knowledge are embedded in that mystery and nowhere else. (Colossians 2:2, *The Message*)

During these special occurrences I have been immersed in His mercy and grace, His patience and truth, His forgiveness and goodness. I am filled with joy—not my own, but the joy of the Lord. His joy is like the golden warmth of the rising sun in early morning; it is as life-giving as spring rain in the desert. Joy is the deep river of God's hope.

One day as Bob and I were driving into town, I spotted a field of blooming bachelor buttons. We stopped, and I waded into a sea

---

[12] Oswald Chambers, *My Utmost For His Highest* (New York: Dodd, Mead, 1963), 362.

[13] James Strong, *The Exhaustive Concordance of the Bible*, The Hebrew and Chaldee Dictionary, p. 116.

of blue with light and dark shades of ultramarine blue, with tiny spots of white and pink. Warmed by the morning sun, the flowers were covered with bees. As a gentle breeze blew across the field, the blue flowers rose and fell in waves. What a sight; it was like being in the midst of wonder. I was so delighted I felt like running and dancing through the flowers. The day of the bachelor buttons is my living experience of joy, so beautiful, so warm, so filled with the rhythm of wind on the sea of flowers and the musical buzz of the bees—a touch of glory, a glimpse of heaven, a celebration of God's creation.

> Therefore with Angels and Archangels, and with all the company of heaven, we laud and magnify thy glorious Name; evermore praising thee, and saying, "Holy, holy, holy, Lord God of Hosts: Heaven and earth are full of thy glory. Glory be to thee, O Lord Most High."[14]

---

[14] *The Book of Common Prayer* (New York: The Church Hymnal Corporation and The Seabury Press, 1977), 334.

Chapter Thirty

Oneness
Woven Together

And the glory which You gave Me I have given them,
that they may be one just as We are one: I in them,
and You in Me; that they may be made perfect in one,
and that the world may know that You have sent Me,
and have loved them as You have loved Me.
—John 17:22-23

October 1, 2011—Today I complete the writing of *Intense Quietness*. Two years ago I began the actual writing of this manuscript after spending some time reviewing my journal notes. I realize this walk has been so great. I can see the Lord truly has increased my ability to spiritually see and hear. He has caused me to live with excited anticipation, thrilled with what might be coming next. My spiritual ear is open to hear His loving whisper, His correction, His observation. With great joy I am thrilled to share the Lord's wondrous work in my life.

———

You, dear Lord, have drawn me deeper and closer into the Father's purposes. Because of Your ongoing guidance, nudges, and enlightenment and Your constant Word that presses me to become filled with Your life, I have gained some inner quietness, an alert stillness. I know, really know You are God and are in control of all circumstances.

Father, Son, and Spirit, all three of You, live in me—a total mystery. You are the One who comes close, who completely identifies with me, enfolding me into the center of Your life. I'm immersed in Your love. My ear is open to hear Your comments, Your take on things. I see delightful things and know they bring You joy. Sometimes I even experience Your compassion for the lost and dying.

Because I'm in You and You are in me, what touches You touches me. Your joy causes me to laugh and be happy. Your Word is woven into me so completely that it corrects me when I'm wrong, it guides me all the time, it encourages me when I'm fainthearted. Prayer is no longer something I do but a continuous conversation. When I awaken in the morning I'm singing Your praise; when I eat, I'm thankful; when I work, You give me strength and integrity; when I rest, my thoughts are of You. Your Spirit prays within me for those needing intercession. Prayer is communion, Spirit to spirit. I'm never alone; You are with me.

Wonders of wonders, I even get to tag along on Your assignments and witness miracles. Walking with You among the living dead, I see people respond in faith to Your love, becoming Your sons and daughters. Sometimes I get to speak Your words of encouragement and touch the brokenhearted. I watch as healing begins. I have great joy when a person actually responds to Your love with thanksgiving and worship.

You have given me a wonderful life. I know it is only Your grace that makes this possible. Quite truthfully my soul still struggles with obedience and unbelief and impatience. Your work is not finished. As You know, I still want what I want when I want it, yet there is another reality springing up in me; a new way of being. Even possessing a tiny speck of Your life changes mine forever. What wonder!

During these last two years I've opened my personal journals and shared bursts and glimpses of the Lord's workings in my life. I hope you, dear friends, who have taken the time to read *The Journey of Intense Quietness* will be profoundly touched by the Holy Spirit.

As I've talked with people, I sense an immense spiritual hunger, a longing for intimacy with the Great Father and Jesus, the beloved Son. I've walked this journey of intense quietness, and I know it leads to the Father. Those who set their hearts to deeply know the Lord will travel this quiet road.

I join the Apostle Paul and pray for you:

> The Father strengthen you by his Spirit—not a brute strength but a glorious inner strength—that Christ will live in you as you open the door and invite him in. And I ask him that with both feet planted firmly on love you'll be able to take in with all Christians the extravagant dimensions of Christ's love. Reach out and experience the breath! Test its length! Plumb the depths! Rise to the heights! Live full lives, full in the fullness of God.

> God can do anything, you know—far more than you could ever imagine or guess or request in your wildest dreams! He does it not by pushing us around but by working within us, his Spirit deeply and gently within us.

> Glory to God in the church!
> Glory to God in the Messiah, in Jesus!
> Glory down all the generations!
> Glory through all millennia! Oh, yes! (Ephesians 3:14-21, *The Message*)

He asks,
Who do you say that I am?
You must answer,
"You are the Great I Am, the Present One, Jesus, the Christ!"
He motions,
Come! Be with Me.